Praise for *We Carry Each Other*

"*We Carry Each Other* is a book for our time. Eric and Sharon Langshur give us a compassionate, caring, and ultimately inspirational look at what we do and say when a loved one or friend is facing serious illness or loss. We learn from the CarePages community and their inspiring stories how to care, how to persevere with grit, and also how to be present with humor, love, and support at a time when our loved ones need us most."
—Steve Case, Chairman and CEO, Revolution Health, cofounder of AOL

"There are miracles we hope for and miracles we dread . . . the first arise from the labors of the mind and body, from perspiration and inspiration and a bit of good luck; the second catch us from behind and push our face into the wall, their miracle is in the grace of love and faith, of the perspiration and inspiration of the heart to break free, it is a teaching in keeping our hearts open in Hell. This fine book is full of such miracles."
—Stephen Levine

"This immensely important book addresses a situation we all will face: how to respond to friends and loved ones who are sick or dying. Feeling inadequate in this situation is normal, but the authors show how inadequacy can be transformed through empathy, compassion, and love into a response that lifts up and sustains the person in need. I know of no other book that so clearly delivers such warm, practical advice for one of the most trying moments we'll ever face. Every family in America should have a copy of *We Carry Each Other.*"
—Larry Dossey, MD, author of *The Extraordinary Healing Power of Ordinary Things*

"*We Carry Each Other* is the perfect title for a book of truly inspired personal stories of everyday, unsung heroes dealing with real life situations. The authors have taken a many times uncomfortable subject, but one most of us will have to deal with in our lifetime, and allowed us a glimpse into our possible future, with hope and dignity. They teach us how to be of help, how to accept and support others in times of need, and how to contact those support groups that can be so essential to our well-being. Don't wait to read this book because you never know when life will expect you to show up and get into action."
—Barb Rogers, author of *Twenty-Five Words*

"*We Carry Each Other* is the resource to help us know what to say, what to do, and how to be when a family member or friend is going through hard times. This book raises care giving to a new level—a journey filled with joy, love, and adventure!"
—Jackie Waldman, author of *The Courage to Give* series

"This is a subject that has been avoided in our culture for much too long. I know the loneliness and isolation that follows the death of a child because people do not know how to respond. This book is a gift that encourages compassion and connection in the most difficult of times."
— Eleanor Wiley, author of *There Are No Mistakes*

"This book so eloquently deals with the pain and the trauma that will visit all of us when we watch, with sadness, the struggle that friends and loved ones face when the unexpected accident or diagnosis is given. The title says it all: *We Carry Each Other.* As Mary Beth Sammons points out in her introduction: 'In the end, all we have is each other. How we learn to carry each other is a secret many of us will spend most of our lives learning.' The commitment that the Langshurs had to helping others when they created CarePages is truly a lifeline for the sick and for those who love them that will live long after most of us who are reading this now. For that, and them, we can all be grateful."
— Karen Casey, author of *Change Your Mind and Your Life Will Follow*

"This volume is a precious gift. It tells unforgettable tales of at once ordinary and extraordinary individuals shoring up spirits and souls, and helps us, by example, find our way through the treacherous terrain of illness and loss. Not only are the intimate stories profoundly inspiring, they are told in beautifully detailed language that carries you through the challenges into the very heart of healing. Even though I have heard myriad tales of hope and have myself experienced the profound power of community, *We Carry Each Other* deeply moved me. This book is destined to become a classic. Even if you're not caring for someone facing major life challenges, this book will reassure you that you will be able to harness the compassion and will to help when a friend or loved one needs you."
— Lori Hope, author of *Help Me Live: 20 Things People with Cancer Want You to Know*

"Gilda Radner once said, 'There are those who open their hearts to others . . . who never think twice about giving of themselves. They are the wonderful, warm-hearted people who make all the difference in our lives.' This is the true essence of *We Carry Each Other,* a heartfelt guide on how to support others by giving of oneself. Eric and Sharon Langshur have taken the compassionate community of CarePages and brought it to life in this book so that we all can learn through the generous spirit and example of others."
— Laura Jane Hyde, CEO, Gilda's Club Chicago

WE CARRY EACH OTHER

GETTING THROUGH LIFE'S TOUGHEST TIMES

Sharon and Eric Langshur *with Mary Beth Sammons*

Foreword by Lee Woodruff, coauthor of *In an Instant:
A Family's Journey of Love and Healing*

Conari Press

First published in 2007 by Conari Press,
an imprint of Red Wheel/Weiser, LLC
With offices at:
500 Third Street, Suite 230
San Francisco, CA 94107
www.redwheelweiser.com

Library of Congress Cataloging-in-Publication Data
Langshur, Sharon.
We carry each other : getting through life's toughest times / Sharon and
Eric Langshur ; with Mary Beth Sammons ; foreword by Lee Woodruff.
p. cm.
ISBN-13: 978-1-57324-311-7 (alk. paper)
ISBN-10: 1-57324-311-6 (alk. paper)
1. Critically ill. 2. Hospital patients. 3. Caregivers. I. Langshur,
Eric. II. Sammons, Mary Beth. III. Title.
R726.8.L36 2007
610—dc22
2007026171

Cover and text design by Jessica Dacher
Typeset in Requiem and Cochin
Cover photograph © Gesundheit /iStockphoto.com

Printed in the United States
TS
10 9 8 7 6 5 4 3 2 1

There's an unspoken rule in our culture that we don't talk about this stuff—illness and death. But intuitively, we know we should, and our impulse is to talk.

—Janet Morahan-Martin, professor of psychology, Bryant University

*To our children, Matthew, Alexander, and Elizabeth for your
inspiration and constant reminder of what is important in life.*

*And to our brother, Mark Day, creator of the very first
CarePage, and to Dr. Amnon Rosenthal, Matthew's cardiologist,
whose encouragement to make CarePages available to
others changed our lives and the lives of so many.*

*We also dedicate this book to our families, who
have always "carried us" through challenging times.*

ACKNOWLEDGMENTS

Today, nearly six hundred leading hospitals and healthcare facilities offer CarePages to their patients and families. If it weren't for the commitment and leadership of these providers, CarePages would not have been possible. We would like to express a debt of gratitude for the trust and confidence these healthcare administrators placed in us and the CarePages service. Together we have touched millions of lives in a very profound way.

We are also deeply grateful to our board of directors, shareholders, and advisors, both formal and informal, who have been a great source of support and counsel in helping us to navigate the complexities of the healthcare industry.

Last, but certainly not least, we extend our heartfelt appreciation to our colleagues—our extended family at CarePages—who come to work each day with a passion for helping others. It is their effort that has made CarePages the outstanding service it is today.

— Eric and Sharon Langshur

CONTENTS

FOREWORD

Not till we are lost, in other words, not till we have lost
the world, do we begin to find ourselves, and realize
where we are and the infinite extent of our relations.
— Henry David Thoreau, *Walden*

Like a thunderclap on an ordinary cloudy day, I was reminded
a few months ago of the thin line between "normal" life and "the
new normal."

My friend and coworker Gretchen called on her way to the
doctor. We went over a few things we had to do for our client that
day. And then she mentioned, with a note of concern in her voice,
that she was on her way to the pediatrician's office. She wanted my
reassurance that her son Liam's disinterest in food was just that; a
three-year-old being famously finicky when it came to eating.

"But ice cream?" she said quizzically when I tried to assuage
her doubts. "Liam loves ice cream."

Fast forward two months. Gretchen and her husband Larry and their fifteen-month-old daughter have virtually moved into Sloan Kettering's pediatric cancer ward as they all valiantly battle a tumor in Liam's abdomen that was so stubborn, so invasive and inoperable at first that he needed multiple chemo treatments just to shrink it to a place where they thought they could perform surgery.

With one diagnosis, on an unsuspecting, deceptively clear blue day, a whole family's life was redefined. An entirely new language of unfamiliar terms and medicalspeak, a battery of nurses and doctors, an army of drugs and medications, procedures and tubes had invaded their formerly predictable life and overturned the familiar routines of diapering and feeding, walks in the stroller, and TV time with *Sesame Street*.

With every crisis, every tragedy, every phone call out of the blue, there is a before and an after. It is a line of demarcation between life as we knew it and life ever after.

My family's own moment came when my husband Bob Woodruff, coanchor of ABC's *World News Tonight* was injured by a roadside bomb while reporting in Iraq. Bob's prognosis was grim. He had suffered a traumatic brain injury as the blast from the bomb had shattered his skull and hundreds of rock shrapnel pieces had been driven into his face and neck. Over the next thirty-six days he lay in a coma. And when he awoke and began the slow journey to heal, I learned just how vividly we do all carry each other.

No one survives a crisis without a web of people—a community of family, friends, and even the power of compassionate strangers. The prayers uttered, the magic crystals and healing stones, the crosses of palm fronds, the books and poems, the loving notes sent: they all helped Bob to heal. I drew strength from the power of touch and hugs and the advice from those who had walked in the shoes of the many that came before them on this awful, brutally human experience.

Bishop Desmond Tutu has a saying that rang true with me when I read it. "I'm sorry to say suffering is not optional. It seems to be part and parcel of the human condition, but suffering can embitter or ennoble."

And so it's how we choose to handle the suffering—to move with grace toward the obstacles and draw on the collective wisdom of others. It doesn't mean that we can't rail against the fates, wring our hands, sob in our good friends arms, or snap inadvertently at the nurses when the frayed rope of our patience is worn to a thin strand.

To me *We Carry Each Other: Getting through Life's Toughest Times* is a manual of invaluable hope for this journey. To read the experiences of others in this book brings comfort and healing. The book is also a reassurance, a beacon to remind us all that we are not alone; that the thoughts, both dark and hopeful, have all been expressed and uttered before.

There is genuine solace in the shared experiences of others. And yet when we undergo a tragedy or a difficult time, we tend to feel as if we are the only people in the world who understand exactly what it feels like to be us. While my husband lay in his coma, his brain grossly swollen beyond his partial skull, I stayed by his side at Bethesda Naval Hospital outside of Washington, D.C. Sleeping in a hotel just a few miles away, hugging my knees in my bed at night, I was petrified of what the future might hold for myself and my four children.

All of the little windows in the apartment buildings and houses around me no longer seemed comforting and filled with bustling, happy lives. Behind each window, I thought, were a million little examples of how your heart could break. In one apartment, I imagined, was a family who'd lost a mother to breast cancer. In the next house, perhaps they were in the throes of a bad divorce or caring for a child with a disability. During the height of my own crisis, I looked at the world with a different filter, as if I had a radar that could see through walls, beyond the corridors of the ICU, and bear witness to one thousand sorrows blooming around me.

As I moved through my days in the hospital, I became keenly aware of all of the well-intentioned actions of those around me. They were offered with love in the hopes of soothing my blind terror, but often they fell short of the mark. Sometimes those around me were tongue-tied, desperate for the right words, the proper thing to do, the appropriate actions.

"Do I call?" I asked myself, when I read a particularly glum e-mail from my friend Gretchen. "Do I ask her how Liam is doing? Does she want to talk about the blood counts, the draining night she had last evening, or does she want to ignore it? Would she rather hear about life outside the hospital walls?" I knew from my own journey that there wasn't always an exact right thing to do and say, nor is every well-intentioned action a totally wrong one.

We can all draw so much knowledge from the pages of this book in terms of how to approach those we love and care for them in ways that support and nurture them. Sometimes those ways of caring seem counterintuitive. But caring in times of crisis and tragedy are not ordinary times. There is no one blueprint that can be applied to every situation, every loved one. In the end, we move by instinct. We follow our guts.

"But how did you deal with the doctors of doom? How did you handle the surgeon fear factor?" Gretchen asked me in despair one day as she had finished listening to yet another medical professional recite her son's sobering odds.

As I formed my own answer, in an effort to talk her down off the ceiling, I thought with amazement that at eighteen months out from our own family crisis I had inadvertently become an expert at navigating these waters. And I thought about the collective wisdom of all of those people who had cared for me. We had all taught each other. I had learned something about the right way to act and the inappropriate ways to react, although the range for both of these was great. And the margin for forgiveness was high—since I understood that most people were woefully ill-equipped to deal with me during my crisis. Often simply being there, being present was enough,

Thankfully, there inevitably comes a period in time when you begin to move away from the eye of the hurricane. No matter what the outcome, you let out your breath and learn to operate once again outside of crisis mode. It's the point in time when the healing begins, when the closure has to start. It's the period when you have to put one tentative foot in front of the other and widen the distance between you and that first horrible piece of news.

We Carry Each Other takes us all right there, to a ringside view of the bedsides and hospital rooms and houses where we meet ordinary people dealing with extraordinary adversity. It provides us with a way not to feel so alone, and it seeks to hand us a road map for navigating and caring for the ones we love by harnessing the collective wisdom and power of a community of resilient caregivers.

Every single person in these stories is a hero, sung or unsung. They are the legions of men and women who hold hope and faith in equal measure. They are the people able to admit that they need others to carry that hope for them from time to time.

People do heal, they do move forward, they do make a life for themselves after the crisis. And that life can be incredibly fulfilling. It's the life of the "new normal."

"First you must touch the black and then move toward the light," was the phrase my friend Vivi, wife of ABC cameraman

Doug Vogt, and I had come up with to help each other when sorrow and despair threatened to overwhelm in the darkest hours of our husbands' injuries. We needed to give each other permission to grieve and be angry. And in that process we learned to extend an arm to pull the other one up again.

I will forever be grateful to Vivi and to the legions of friends and family who used their wisdom and their instincts to take care of me in the wake of Bob's injury. Vivi and I would have lapped up the many nuggets contained on these pages. Perhaps if we'd had this book, we might have been easier on ourselves on certain days. I carried her. She carried me. In the end, we all carry each other.

Lee Woodruff

Mary Beth's Story

His name was Henry. We met, in a way, the night he was hit and killed by a motorist in front of my suburban Chicago home.

It has been several years since that brutally bitter January evening. Yet even today the haunting image, the aftershock, reverberates in my mind.

A deep feeling grips my chest as I remember the moment I raced out of my house and found him there, a lump of black overcoat flattened to the pavement, life draining out of him in a pool of blood. "Oh my God," I remember thinking. "Please don't let him die." Then, dropping to my knees and bending over him. I'd learn later he had been thrown and landed on his skull. I found his black shoe the next day in the snow in my front yard. But now, all I remember is a terrifying fear and helplessness, screaming (inside . . . I couldn't get the words out),

"Help! Somebody, help!" It must have been only minutes, but it seemed like hours. I knelt there, held his hand, trying to breathe life into him with my words: "I'm here. I'm here." And praying/mandating, "God, be here, be here *now.*"

He died moments after the paramedics arrived.

One minute I am cooking dinner for my three children, making plans for carpools to basketball practice and ballet, and figuring out how to orchestrate three parent-teacher conferences at conflicting times. The next I am kneeling on the pavement at the side of a stranger, horrified, scared, and learning firsthand about death throes as his spirit escaped.

Since that night, illness and death have come knocking at my door and ripping through my house like a tornado. In the past year, I feel like I've turned into an episode on *Saturday Night Live* and I am Debbie Downer, ticking off a checklist of sickness and death. Only no one is laughing. As much as I try, I can't seem to heal, free, and cheer up my friends and relatives who are being pushed to the very edge of life.

There is no sugarcoating this, except to say that I am at a point in my life where the right words spoken at the right time are crucial. The challenges of the past year have overwhelmed me and at times brought what seems like inconsolable grief. Vince, our fifty-one-year-old next-door neighbor and my children's "uncle/guardian angel," died suddenly in his sleep of a heart arrhythmia. Our funny, joyous friend Ann, a thirty-seven-year-old mom of three, died from ovarian cancer just weeks before the first birthday of her youngest child. My tenderhearted friend Cara, who had compassion for others like no one you could imagine, battled for her life, isolated most days in the cancer ward of a Chicago hospital. In December 2006, she lost her battle with leukemia, and now she is gone and I can barely hold the sorrow. Last summer, while my friend Pam and her husband Bill were driving on a rural Wisconsin road on vacation, a car ran through a stop sign, smashing into their SUV. Pam is my exercise buddy. Last summer, I helped push her wheelchair, then her walker to our outings at Starbucks. Last month I went to a fund-raiser for my cousin Patrick. He's forty-seven, a father of two who has stage four cancer. At the fund-raiser in the alley of an Irish pub, our clan gathered as a priest renewed Patrick's and Mary's vows and all we cousins cried.

I don't know what to say. I don't know what to do to make any of these situations better. I want to see my friends and family smile again, and laugh.

As a forty-something single mom of three teens and the only sibling living on the same side of the country as my parents, I find myself constantly pulled—racing from the school gym where my freshman daughter, Emily, is playing volleyball to the bedsides of my dad and mom. Both have spent most of the past two years tethered to machines, fighting blood clots, pneumonia, and tricky cancers at a suburban Chicago hospital.

All of these events have jolted me into action and into a desire to transform the times of sorrow into lessons that can help carry others and help people like us carry our friends and loved ones through the hurts. All of my friends have faced their misfortune with grace, class, wit, and unconquerable spirits. In sharing their journeys with me, they have been teaching me many lessons about the vulnerability of us all. What I do know is that disaster, illness, and loss bring a strange, instant kinship. Suddenly, you are moving in one direction, then *boom*, real life happens and your world is turned upside down.

In the death of my neighbor, in the loss of my friends, in the eyes of my aging parents, I have seen the fragility of life. I know the exquisite bond we all share. I've tried to make sense of my being there with a stranger who died in my arms one evening. He never gained consciousness. But, somehow, in a deep part of my being where I know my soul resides, I feel he knew that *he was not alone*, that his widow would find some solace in the fact that *he was not alone*. And, I would make peace with the fact that though I couldn't save him, I didn't leave him there to die alone.

Standing in the face of so much serious illness and loss, I have found myself and my universe of friends and family around me challenged to make a choice: to become better by taking action or to walk away. Growing up, my parents always taught me—by example, not words—the importance of being there for others when they need us, with sensitivity and compassion. I have tried to make it better, to be present through the toughest challenges, but still the questions tug:

What do I say? What do I do?

How can I help?

Why do some people have the gift for enduring in the face of illness when the odds seem to be stacked against them?

What is the secret to a deep knowing some people have that keeps them steadfast in the toughest times, through the deepest loss?

How can we stand strong against life's storms and be tender at the same time?

How do some people keep their spirits alive when everything around them seems to be withering?

There are no right or wrong answers. Our society certainly has little to offer. Clichés such as "I know how you feel" and "It will get better" just don't seem to work. "Is there anything I can do to help?" is surprisingly unhelpful sometimes. People often don't know what to do, so they don't do anything. And that, I discovered, can be the worst choice. Crises can be tests of love and friendship, and it is often surprising who steps up and who steps back.

In looking for ways to bring comfort and support, I went on a mission to find tools. As a journalist, I make my living searching high and low for "the best" sources, the ordinary people who are making an extraordinary difference in the lives of others. I looked and looked and looked for people who instinctively knew how to respond to friends and loved ones in need.

I'd like to call it fate or serendipity, but after exhaustive e-mail missives, phone calls, and unsuccessful trips to bookstores for the answers, two things happened. I received an e-mail from a colleague asking if I knew a technology developer. A company in Chicago that creates online support communities for patients in hospitals across the country—CarePages—was growing and needed more tech people. Later that day, I received a call from my friend Cara. She was crying and calling from the tenth floor of Rush Medical Center in Chicago which, unbeknownst to any of us at the time, would become her home for the next eleven months. She needed a community of supporters.

And that's when I met Eric and Sharon Langshur, founders of CarePages, and the incredible team who have made giving support, reaching out, and growing community for thousands of people in hospitals across the world a priority and a passion. The Langshurs founded *CarePages.com* after their own son, Matthew, was diagnosed with a chronic heart condition and underwent three open-heart surgeries before his second birthday. Today, it's the largest online social network and support community of its kind in the world, serving more than 600 hospital systems and nearly 2 million patients and their families. CarePages is a place people turn to in illness or loss. There, people find hope, community, and emotional support.

Cara liked the idea of being able to connect with her huge circle of friends and family via e-mail and grabbed on like a lifeline to the opportunity to create her CarePage, "CaringforCara." For months, friends and family wrapped their arms around her and supported her with prayers and messages there, especially during the times when she was in isolation and not able to have visitors. And, we were able to have some fun and lightness too. Always in pursuit of cute guys, we tried to turn living in a hospital into a great way for Cara to meet her own Dr. McDreamy of Rush Medical Center. At one point, we staged a contest and posted photos of the top runners in the Cara-meets-a-doc contest.

When she lost her beautiful auburn hair, she posted different looks—Dolly Parton hair, among others—and asked us to vote on a replacement "do." Throughout, we learned by following the lead of Cara's considerable wit—matched by none—and humor, which became the key to caring for Cara. During the days before she died, her circle of 100-plus friends wrote letters on her CarePage telling her how her life had impacted theirs. It was a touching testimonial to a woman who made such a difference in the lives of so many. It allowed those who loved her to surround her in caring and compassion. She was not alone in her final moments.

And so, that is what this book is all about: a chance to meet people like Cara, who can inspire us all to care more. Here we share stories of dozens of patients and families who have endured illness and loss and found others who stepped up gracefully to surround them in love and care. We hope that by having a glimpse of their situations, *you* will be better able to figure out the best ways to respond to friends in need.

Through interviewing people and helping write these stories, we have learned many things I wish I had known when the tragedies I described came hurling through my life. Our friends and their stories are not unique. But their experiences have taught us this: we have to learn to *carry each other.*

In this book, I serve as narrator, observer, participant—sharing some of my own stories and those that have emerged through the vision of what the CarePages founders, Sharon and Eric, have created and the unique community of people who have gained knowledge from the things they have experienced and endured. These are stories of the irrepressible human spirit. We share them with you with the hope that you will find some shared experience with these friends and a truth that will empower you and your loved ones to carry each other and to keep on carrying on.

As we were conducting the interviews and writing the stories, the question always emerged: "Why write these stories?"

Right before Cara died, I found the answer. I was at the hospital where Cara was in the ICU, tethered to a ventilator and dozens of tubes that coursed insulin, antibiotics, and who knows what else through her body. She was semiconscious, and the doctors used percentages—as in 10 percent by the end of the week—to describe what her chances would be.

There are times in our lives when we want desperately and secretly to do something perfect. This was one. Instead, I just stood silently for a long time at Cara's bedside, holding on to her arm and hand and not knowing if she really was in a coma and knew I was there. I felt like a total dolt, so inept and vulnerable and not knowing what to say or do to help her. I remember how, early on in her illness, I had found this Irish prayer for her about *anam caras* (soul friends; she loved the fact that *Cara* translated to "friend"). According to the *anam cara* Celtic tradition, prayer is the act of sending out the light and goodness from yourself to your *anam caras*. So for a long, long time that night, I just clung onto her arm, as if by holding on tight I could breathe new life into her and help her heal, to help her be free of her pain and make her smile and laugh again.

In my past I have been known to be shy about telling people how much I really care. I think they will somehow intuit my feelings, and later I look back, wishing I had mustered up the courage to share. I decided I needed to tell Cara how much she has meant in my life and in the lives of my children and our circle of friends, and to talk to her just as I would if we were on our way to a Cubs game and discussing our latest crushes and our silly exploits. I talked, I tried to laugh, and I cried. I'm sure the medical staff buzzing by the curtain of her room thought I was a nutcase babbling away as I was. But four hours into my visit, Cara looked at me, a tear streaming down her cheek. I reached out and wiped it away and told my friend how much I loved her.

I'm not sure if I helped Cara, but the grace of that moment awakened something in me. I knew she knew she was not alone. I will always remember and be grateful for her friendship and for the love she poured out to everyone she met. Cara and the circle of friends we share came into my life when something had hurt me very badly. She offered the warmth of her friendship, even on days when I wasn't exactly someone to be loved. I write this book to carry on her legacy of caring in the hope that it will help you shine the light of your love and friendship on someone else who is feeling fragile.

That is the "why" of writing these stories: to call out to others, to help you make contact with others, to break the silence about "what do we do or say." "How do we move to another's side in times of pain and anguish?" Our hope is that you will share these stories, and they will inspire you to help someone else stay afloat, to reach for them and to keep us all above the water.

In the end, all we have is each other. How we learn to carry each other is a secret many of us will spend most of our lives learning. I hope these stories help you carry yourself and someone else through the storms and let them know they are not alone.

Mary Beth Sammons

ERIC AND SHARON'S STORY

When our son Matthew was born in 1998, we thought we knew all we'd need to know about health care, if not parenting. Sharon was a pediatrician. We were both healthy, active professionals and were never really "sick." And then Matthew was born with a congenital heart defect. He required three open-heart surgeries in the first months of his life, and our lives suddenly seemed to be nothing but hospitals and health care. Our family created a "CarePage" Web site to keep friends and family updated on his condition and realized that we came to depend on the messages from friends and family for encouragement and support. By the time of Matthew's third surgery, his site was receiving more than 2,000 hits a day.

Soon after that, though, we were at a crossroads. Matthew was recovering and our lives could have gone on largely as they were before. Or, we could take what we'd learned from this experience and help others. We could turn the horrible experience into something positive. Matthew's cardiologist at the University of Michigan urged us to use our talents—Eric as a business leader and Sharon as a pediatrician—to create support networks for other patients and their families so that they would also never be alone. Thus, the genesis of CarePages.

We wanted our experience with Matthew's CarePage not to be confined just to those people who knew his story. We wanted everyone who faced a medical event to feel—and you really can—the power that comes from a community of support, even one online.

Now, we want to do more. *You* are the reason *We Carry Each Other* exists. Your everyday hopes, the dreams you have for loved ones and the struggle to find meaning and clarity of purpose in life challenges—whether physical, emotional, or spiritual—come alive on these pages as you show us how to carry each other.

For some of you, the happy hopes exploded the day you stood next to your loved one, looked in the doctor's eyes, and saw that something was wrong. For others, the news came in the wee hours of the morning, a phone call that jolted you from sleep with the directive to race to an emergency room. A collapse from a sudden heart attack. A shadow on a CAT scan. An automobile accident. Suddenly, the world you knew was turned upside down. The life of someone you love was pushed against the maw.

We have met many of you in the heart of crisis and emotional loss, when at first it seemed the world you knew was shattered.

On our Internet pages, you had the courage to confront the sobering realities: the diagnosis of cancer of a six-month-old who three days after her first birthday lost her battle; the mom who six months later cries, "When is it going to stop hurting?" And, then moves to "What can I do to help other parents?"

These days, less than a year after the death of their infant, she and her husband walk other parents through the struggle and inspire them to live through the pain and move on.

That's where the impetus for this book comes from. Our CarePages community members asked us for more, to help them figure out what to do to help friends and families through hard times. There's a lot you can do to make things better. Through the eyes and ears of our members who have shared their stories, we hope we have created a definitive resource on "what to say and what to do" when you or a loved one suffers illness or loss.

The book brings readers onto the front lines, at the bedsides and into the living rooms and offices of ordinary people dealing with extraordinary adversity. CarePage members and others have shared their stories and inspired a phenomenon that is driving a social movement of compassionate caring for people who are struggling themselves or caring for a loved one facing illness, loss, and life's difficulties. This is much like how the book *Random Acts of Kindness* brought worldwide attention to simple acts of goodness.

We Carry Each Other uses anecdotes from real life to offer ways we can support friends, colleagues, and loved ones who are struggling with illness or loss. The stories show over and over again how much we can make a difference in someone else's life. And, they show us how our words and actions can transform us as well.

Through our CarePages community, we talked to hundreds of people who have triumphed under unthinkable adversity and those who have wrapped them in their compassion and caring. We have collected their voices and human experiences.

These healing and inspiring stories are tangible and real. They give meaning to the toughest challenges and allow us to connect to one another's souls and spirits. For the person who is ill or experiencing loss, sharing the story gives meaning to the journey. For the rest of us, they inspire us: Yes, we can make a difference. Yes, there are many ways we can help someone. Here, in this book, we offer a guide through the use of some powerful examples.

Illness often intensifies feelings of isolation. These feelings can be worsened by a lack of communication and community. But the experiences also can be transformative. We share the stories of ordinary people living ordinary lives that overnight become broken, but who have connected to each other's souls and spirits to become partners in healing. *We Carry Each Other* addresses the spiritual issues of challenge—meaning, love, faith, courage, hope, and compassion—in the language of those who face it and live it every day on the front lines through their life experiences.

The book looks at the practical, the profound, the reassuring, and the humorous ways to respond in the toughest situations. This book is like group support—a place where people can feel safe enough to talk about what is really going on in their struggles and to share with you, the reader, ideas for helping. We hope it will inspire you to make some simple gestures—for yourself and others—that can make a big difference.

The stories you will find here are those of people who have faced pain and sorrow head-on and of the people who have stood at their sides. Together, they have found hope to move through the darkest hours to transformation and new beginnings. We humbly suggest that reading about such people—people who learned to *carry each other*—can open your hearts to greater healing.

Welcome,
Eric and Sharon Langshur

CHAPTER I

WHAT CAN I DO WHEN HARD TIMES HIT?

Challenged by the Hurt of a Loved One,
We Are Called to Compassion and Caring

Faith in the future is not dead in our hearts.
Better still, it is this hope, deepened and
purified, Which seems bound to save us.
— Pierre Teilhard de Chardin

Throughout the dark night, when the call comes in—"Vince has died in his sleep," "I'm sorry your dad's cancer has spread," "There's been a car accident, your son is in the hospital"—we are called on to be companions in the darkness, to move fluidly to the sides of our loved ones as they struggle against the dimming light. Sometimes we feel like deer in the headlights. But, the moment comes when we walk into a hospital room and our mom or dad or friend or neighbor looks into our eyes with a quiet nakedness of desperation and truth, and we *know* we are called to be present. At that moment, something seeps into our souls and grace steps in. For me, the way through is a sustaining faith and a belief in the connectedness of all of us.

From out of the shadow of the darkness, we are called on to emerge in these unsettling days to carve out a space of safety and protection, a place to breathe for those who are experiencing pain that can't be hidden, hurt that won't stop aching, for loss that severs. Out loud, or only in the protection of their hearts, they call out to us: "I can't do it this time, the pain, the pain," as Martha Popson describes in her prayer "Survivor."

"Mom has advanced esophageal cancer and a dismal one-year survival rate of less than 5 percent." "Your son is in the hospital. It is a car accident." We can take some comfort that illness and loss are part of the natural order of things. But how do we respond when we get the call from a friend in the hospital saying it is leukemia? Regardless of our true feelings, what do we do to help that person make it through their ordeal?

How do we catch the vision to see the dark and to move with someone into it as they experience it?

What do we do to become fully aware and attentive to their cries for help? Or to know we are needed when our friends or family don't know how to ask for our help?

What is the grace that blesses us and gives us the strength and courage to experience another's anguish and pain with them, to move to their side with confidence?

There are good sound reasons to answer these questions, to ponder the mystery of why we need to carry each other. The mystery is always in the next question. But the answer is always the same: Because we have to. Because we are called on to carry each other. Because when we love someone, we promise: You are never alone.

Quotes to Inspire You to Take Action, to Care

"Too many of us panic in the dark. We don't understand that it's a holy dark and that the idea is to surrender to it and the journey through to real light."
—Sue Monk Kidd

"For me, the darkness is partially summed up in the word 'question.' I feel wrapped in an awful, silent pondering that doesn't know any answers, only questions."
—Thomas Merton

"I had prepared for an approaching sorrow, but not, as it turned out, the one that was nearest."
—Carole Radziwill, author of *What Remains: A Memoir of Fate, Friendship & Love*

"In the dark times, the eye begins to see. The dark times in life are not our enemy. Dark times empty the world of things that would otherwise distract us from seeing the important things. Enter the darkness with confidence."
—Theodore Roethke

A Circle of Friends
They Answered the Call in the Night

What we need is one greater, wiser, and stronger than
ourselves, who can also become little and enter into
us and then expand and strengthen us.
—Jack Shea

It is hard to know how we will respond when difficulties and mis-
fortunes come knocking at our door. It seems there is always the
possibility of sinking in despair, of giving up, of becoming bitter
or angry and living life based on fear. But when Baadrea Bagley
got the worst call of her life—that her son, Brandon, had been in
a horrible automobile accident, she had no choice, she says, but to
believe in the power of hope. And so, when friends rallied at her
side, she let them be the cloak of resilience and strength to emerge
out of tragedy and live focused on what can be, instead of what
was taken away in the accident.

Baadrea Bagley will never forget the night she heard the
news. Two days before, on the night the world learned actor
Christopher Reeve had died from medical complications from
his 1995 riding accident, Baadrea's son Brandon Aitchison had
pulled her aside and told her he was afraid: "I don't know what I
would do if I was ever paralyzed and couldn't walk," the twenty-
year-old avid snowboarder and water skier confided.

On October 12, 2004, the Denver, Colorado, college student,
who lived life in high gear, was headed for the library to study
for midterms. His cell rang with a call from buddies who were
headed up to the mountains for a little four-wheeling.

"I knew it would be a good time, and I needed a break from my
history notes," says Brandon. "We got up there and had our fun
tossing it up in the mud. Next thing I know I'm lying in the car

on my back looking up at the floor with water and blood dripping from the upside down seats in front of me thinking, 'Well, it looks like we rolled.'"

Four days later, he woke up again as doctors at Boulder Community Hospital said the q-word: *quadriplegic.*

"I woke to the sounds of beeping machines and had tubes coming out of me every which way," says Brandon, now twenty-one. "Not being able to move didn't come to me as a surprise; it's as if I already knew and accepted it. I yelled, calling for anyone who could hear me. In no time my mom was right there to comfort me and that was all I needed. I had no idea what was next for me."

For Baadrea, recalling what it felt like to confront her son's mortality is a nightmare only a parent can understand. This couldn't happen to her son; he was her baby, central to her life and the lives of their family and his own circle of friends. "The call changed my life forever," says Baadrea.

That night she had just returned from a rare "Girls Night Out" with her friends and was just putting her head on the pillow when the phone rang at 10 P.M.

"Your son has been in an accident and he has very significant injuries," she remembers someone telling her. As her husband, Brandon's stepdad, raced them through the mountains and the 25-minute ride to the hospital, Baadrea says all she can remember is crying out, "Oh God, oh God, please, please help my son."

For the next nine hours, she paced the halls of the hospital as surgeons fought to save her son's life.

"I don't smoke, but I wanted a cigarette," she says. "There was this victim's advocate who kept following me around everywhere I went. I mean I couldn't even go to the bathroom. I know they're probably trained, but I felt like I was on suicide watch. I just wanted to say, 'Go away.'"

Instead, she snuck into the hospital chapel, got down on her knees, let the tears stream out. "And then I got up, wiped them off, and said, 'My life has changed. I have a different mission now, and God, I am ready for it.'"

And then they came: friends, relatives, Baadrea's friends and Brandon's. They set up tables of food and brought tents to camp out overnight so Baadrea and her husband, Hal, and son, Spenser—Brandon's younger brother—were never alone. Brandon's friends flew in from colleges across the country and pulled up sleeping bags for the giant caring campout. Huge care packages arrived stuffed with magazines, food, tea, and lotions—everything hospital campers would need so they would not have to go home and replenish for three weeks.

"We had a giant slumber party at the hospital," says Baadrea. "Relatives flew in from California and we were embraced with love in so many ways, I still cry thinking about it.

"Friends and family stayed with us around the clock at the hospital. They were our protectors, our supporters, and then they became our bridge to the new life—the life after the accident. We were never alone."

When Brandon eventually moved home, the steady stream of his teen club arrived daily to watch rented movies and sit everpresent with their buddy.

"They dropped everything in their lives to be with Brandon," says Baadrea. "Honestly, I expected that they would all disappear, that they would be freaked out by this. But they stayed at his side."

And that is what she did every day for months after the accident. She stood at her son's side and helped him pursue the small victories—removing the ventilator, learning to feed himself with a special device, dress, bathe, and live independently, moving into a two-story house with two of his college buddies in Denver, where he is a student and a House of Representatives communications intern at the Capitol.

Brandon says, "People ask me, if I could go back in time would I change things, and my response is always 'No.' What if I hadn't gotten in the car? What if I had been in the front seat? I could choose to think about 'what ifs' but what would that accomplish? I would always be running those thoughts in my head, so instead I think about *what is* and that is that I'm still alive.

Words to Live By

"She snuck into the hospital chapel, got down on her knees, let the tears stream out. 'And then I got up, wiped them off, and said, 'My life has changed. I have a different mission now, and God, I am ready for it.'"

"I have learned to adapt to my situation as it's happening right now. I have learned to sometimes use my teeth in place of my left hand. I try not to think about what I don't have but what I do have. I have been blessed with the return of movement in my right leg, my right hand, my weak left leg, and control of my bladder. It is sometimes hard to see the people around me being able to walk without thought or use their hands without limitations, but I quickly replace those thoughts with the thoughts of where I came from—lying on a hospital bed not being able to move at all—and I am filled with thankfulness."

Recently he told his mom, who was a tad worried about his new living arrangements, "Mom, don't worry, I'll figure it out."

The Call to Care for Our Parents

By Mary Beth Sammons

Life doesn't accommodate you. . . . It shatters you.
We must all sit in the ground glass of our illusions.
—Florida Scott Maxwell, *The Measure of My Days*

So many things come to you when you are forced to look deep inside for the answers. In caring for my own parents as their health begins to slide downhill, I have found myself reaching inside to the memories and circumstances of my childhood—the times when I felt sick or I saw my parents taking care of their parents or a friend or relative.

It is perhaps irony, for sure grace, that as our parents face the countdown to the last years of their lives, and we begin to face our own mortality, we look to the memories and light that they brought to our lives. I'm learning how to care for my mom and dad, by remembering how they cared for me.

Although almost every one of us will at some point face the inevitability of caring for—and perhaps burying—our parents, some of us, namely me, aren't so great at helping our moms and dads through it. Kevin O'Connor, OSP, a pastoral counselor and educator at Loyola University in Chicago, thinks it is important for those of us who are struggling with caring for our parents to come up with a game plan and to realize from the get-go that it is going to be an intense experience. And just think of it: the elderly population is expected to grow by 75 percent in the next thirty years.

So, what is the solution for the person who's mired in "the Sandwich Generation," who is caught in between taking care of our children and our parents?

Maybe some of the answers lie in the struggle to juggle. People have different responses to caring for their parents, and doing so is hard. I know. Sometimes we have ambivalent feelings. Joan Walsh Anglund wrote, "Adversity often activates a strength we did not know we had." I think that speaks volumes about what it is like to care for aging parents and our children. What helps me is knowing that just by taking action and caring we are carrying our parents and helping them to know they are not alone.

The best thing my mother taught me was that good mothers are supposed to feed anyone who is sick steaming chicken noodle soup with crackers spread with peanut butter and tea with honey. I've done that fairly well for my children. And I'm not trying to boast, but I'm pretty good at answering the call for ailing neighbors, friends, and coworkers, too. But though I am good at caring for many others, I am paralyzed when it comes to knowing what to do for my parents. I proclaim myself a struggling novice and brutal failure. I can't seem to do this caregiving tradition backward, reversed. I'm scared watching my parents get sick and old. I'm scared thinking I am getting old.

Now that my mother and father are eighty, I am summoned—often—to a now all-too-familiar ER thirty miles away and the uncertainty that waits at the other end of the middle-of-the-night, mid-hair appointment, or mid-treadmill phone call. I know several ER docs by first name and an anesthesiologist who waves to me in the hospital cafeteria. I have mastered the art of maintaining a career via cell phone and laptop by stepping outside the electronic hospital doors and making conference calls on the freeway.

It's much more difficult to witness my parents bedridden than it was to take care of my son when he was hospitalized at three. The reality that my parents are part of this vulnerable population of the extremely sick and old teaches me how little I really know about caring for other human beings—especially ones who once cared for me.

Some days I feel like I'm right on the mark when I've cornered a doctor in the hall and pinned down the results of the test and the graveness of the word *shadow* in my dad's lungs. Or, the days when I can keep my dad laughing despite the sharp and sudden pains that punctuate his every cough. I need to remember that despite the traffic and juggling, it is important for me to provide door-to-door service on an especially difficult day in outpatient chemo.

But many times, I feel frustrated that I'm not doing enough, both at home for my kids and in the hospital room. I come home drained, as if I am the one who should be sick from the chemotherapy, and feel guilty when I'm dialing for pizza instead of whipping up a spring chicken scaloppini and spinach salad. Usually, I'm totally at a loss for what to do or say when my dad is calling out in pain for a nurse or my mom is lying there paralyzed in fear of what the five different specialists have told her that day and looks at me for the answers.

"It will be so restful," I lamely told my dad the day they told him he would have to live temporarily in a rehab center (translated in his mind as "nursing home"). It frightened me to see him cry when he begged me not to send him. Taking on the role of the permanent fall guy didn't time out right for me, especially when I had decided I could finally have a life in a mere five or ten years when all my kids' teen years were over.

All their lives they sheltered me and my siblings. Last Christmas Eve, my sister flew in from California and we moved our parents to a teeny one-bedroom place at the retirement community. I was trying to be unsentimental and positive when I exclaimed, "This is going to be such an opportunity for you."

For a long time, they insisted they could still drive—until the ugly reality of the day my father "accidentally" drove three hours out of the way and got lost in another state while on a well-traveled route. I've discovered it's easier to take car keys away from a sixteen-year-old who broke a rule than it is your parents, and, as their chauffeur, I know what it is like to live in doctors' waiting rooms and outpatient labs watching the chemo drip.

I've learned to shift gears—fast. And, I'm not afraid to say that my experience is just part of a trend that I project will affect most of my peers during the next few decades. But it's a trend in which the consequences remain uncertain. I'm part of a generation of women who spent the past twenty-one years guilt wracked over how much we worked or didn't work, breast-fed or bottle-fed, and suffered free-floating anxiety over McDonald's as dinner after soccer. I live a life that is a fragile mix of seeming like I have it together, then watching it all fall apart.

As someone who is usually outspoken, I find my silence around the answers and fragile understanding of how to care for my aging parents confusing and scary. Sometimes in the hospital elevators I look at the other visitors bearing stacks of crossword puzzle books and flowers to find hints that will explain the ways we're all in this together. I'm hoping that there are some answers on how to do this better, so that it feels a little less crazy.

Mostly, I think I'm looking for my mom to show me the recipe for chicken soup for the senior when she doesn't even remember my name. I don't know the answers, but I do know most of my peers these days are asking these same questions.

You've Got to Have Friends
by Kevin O'Conner

I've found the best solutions come from talking to others who are in my situation. Important things to remember:

+ One friend reminds me that we all need support.
+ Another has hired a home health care aide to help ease her workload and relieve some of the stress of taking care of aging parents.
+ Another friend recommends checking the local newspaper for caregiving support networks.
+ It's important to take care of those around us, yes, and it's also important to take care of *ourselves*.

Tips on Caring for Your Parents—and Keeping Your Sibling Relationships

+ Open communication as wide as possible, at least within your immediate family.
+ Resist the temptation to fight.
+ If one sibling is a nurse, doctor, or premed student, give that person the role of communicating with the professionals, but insist that she not make decisions without consulting the rest of you.
+ Use influential words; avoid pathetic words.
+ Ask for help—specific help.
+ Don't do too much, especially if you are the responsible one in the family—share the load.
+ If there are bridges that need to be repaired, consider doing only enough to allow communication now—don't attempt a complete reconciliation while mom and dad are struggling.
+ When money is involved, seek outside advice, even if your brother is an accountant and your sister is a lawyer.

→ Getting Started: The Inside Track on Carrying Each Other

The reality is that you, or someone you know, maybe the person sitting in the cubicle next to you, could receive one of these calls, any day, anytime, soon. Maybe you already have and you know what it is like to be faced with struggling to supervise your loved one's care and work duties simultaneously. Not to mention trying to make life "normal" for other children or family members. And yourself.

Illness, disease, and disability turn everything upside down. But whatever changes you, a friend, or a loved one faces, you still have the spirit inside that needs to be nourished, and true feelings are sure to emerge. It may be the first time you are confronting the relationship and asking what it means. Anger, sadness, fear, resentment for what appears to be an obligation, or a burning desire to connect in a deep way with your loved one—all of these are okay and normal.

Don't be hard on yourself. The call to care can rock your world and sometimes be devastating. Generally, most people do feel vulnerable and out of control. Others might find comfort in talking about it. If you are afraid, the first step is to admit it. And if you don't know what to do, check out some of the creative ways in this book that people have reached out to care.

We believe these thoughtful and compassionate behaviors are certain to inspire. Just like all of these people in these stories, we each have our own unique ways of responding or reaching out. But what we've learned is that ultimately the only way to respond is to take that first step and do something.

Tips for Helping a Friend or Loved One Who Is Hurting

Right after you get the call:

+ Put your compassion in writing. One of the best ways to express concern is to send an e-mail or short note that says, "I'm thinking of you," or, "You are not alone. I care."
+ Or call and admit, "I don't know what to say. But I care."
+ Try not to make assumptions. Don't say, "I know exactly how you feel," or, "This is the best thing that could happen, you'll see."
+ Don't rush in with advice. Resist the temptation to dish out a list of "You shoulds."

For a friend who is seriously ill:

+ If she is mobile, take her out for coffee, or just a ride in the car, so she won't feel so isolated.
+ Don't overstay your visit.
+ If she's a close friend, volunteer to clean her house, drive her kids, or drive her to physical therapy or doctor's appointments.
+ Organize a meals-on-wheels delivery among friends and family to bring dinner every night.
+ Be aware that sometimes he may need to talk, other times he won't.
+ Start a prayer circle when appropriate, where friends can gather to pray for your friend.

♥ From the CarePages Frontlines

Carrying Your Adult Children through Cancer

"I was shocked to hear my daughter had breast cancer. She was just twenty-eight years old. I wanted to do my best to support her, so after the mastectomy I helped with cleaning and laundry, but I didn't want to take over. I thought it was important for her husband and two daughters to feel they were doing their part as well. My role was to listen to her, support her decisions regarding treatment choices, and help get answers to the questions that arose."
— *Gail Nagel*

Checking In from College: A Daughter Rallies the Troops for Her Mom

"Four years ago I was diagnosed with breast cancer. My daughter was a college student studying nursing over 1,500 miles away. She would draw pictures, take photos of her friends dressed up, and make other little things I could carry with me while I was in treatment. She also contacted some of my friends, who sent me drawings and other little gifts—'coupons' I could call them for—'one hour of tea drinking,' 'grocery shopping'—they would come to my home, get the list, and take me along if I had the energy—'gardening coupon'—weed my garden or whatever outside yard work I wanted or needed done—I felt loved and cherished, and we continued the 'coupons' because unfortunately I was the first in my group of friends to be diagnosed with breast cancer."
— *Carmen Ailes*

CHAPTER 2

Moving into the Unknown

Finding Strength in Our Vulnerability and Embracing Change

The call to care for another person is a yearning from the heart to live beyond ourselves. But this call sometimes seems overwhelming, and we're tempted to look the other way. "Not now, I just got done getting my kids through their teen years, and now my mom is sick." "I can't deal with funerals. I'm not good at them." "I've never been a widow, what am I possibly supposed to say or do that doesn't sound stupid or superficial?"

Caring, reaching outside of ourselves, is also scary—love, compassion, and service to others don't come without risk. It's a risk to reach out of ourselves and respond to the suffering of others.

But the truth is, whatever we do—big or small—creates ripples of caring. And somewhere inside of ourselves, we all possess a deep longing to give and care. It is at times of extreme challenge that we discover new things about ourselves and those around us. Sometimes our own compassion and that of others surprise us. Here, through these stories, we find a road map to guide us.

Brave Heart
Breaking the Silence to Open to Real Caring and Compassion
By Jim Moon

Compassion for me is just what the word says it is: it is "suffering with." It is an immediate participation in the suffering of another to such a degree that you forget yourself and your own safety and act spontaneously.
—Joseph Campbell

The silence surrounding illness often becomes deafening. What is not said, not addressed, can become the painful block to authentic caring.

Here, Jim Moon, a San Francisco graphic designer, shares a moment that transformed his view of what it means to make sure someone you love is not alone and to be present in caring.

Many years ago, dating back to my corporate days, one of our group vice presidents, Bud Hess, was diagnosed with cancer. It was serious, and I think it became clear early on that it was unlikely he would survive. Bud was very well liked. This made his illness much more difficult to bear emotionally and just about impossible to understand. Here was a guy that took exceptional care of all his employees and *he* was going to die.

Throughout his struggle, he continued to visit our corporate offices in San Francisco. Each time he was in town everyone could plainly see his deteriorating condition. But Bud always managed to put on a pretty convincing show of strength.

Toward the end, however, it was clear that the disease was getting the best of him.

On his last visit, a number of us were talking to Bud. The conversation addressed everything but the obvious. Everyone, including Bud, was trying to avoid the painful truth that he was struggling.

Words to Live By

"One person sliced through all the small talk and asked in plain, unfiltered English, 'Bud, how are your treatments going?' We all got a chance to tell Bud how sorry we were about his illness and to wish him well. I think he knew at that moment how much we all cared for him and that he was not alone."

One person sliced through all the small talk and asked in plain, unfiltered English, "Bud, how are your treatments going?"

There was a deafening silence, and then Bud began to answer the question. Everyone instantly dropped their distance and listened. More questions were asked and answered. We all got a chance to tell Bud how sorry we were about his illness and to wish him well. I think he knew at that moment how much we all cared for him and that he was not alone.

I have always been grateful to my colleague and friend Chris Morgan for having the courage to approach the subject in the first place. Chris raised all boats, not only for Bud, but for all of us who where engaged in the conversation.

This small human exchange didn't save Bud. But, I bet it did lift his spirits more than a little. One brave person broke the silence that triggered a genuine display of warmth and concern.

Speak What Matters
Calls Connect in a Wonderful and Mysterious Way

There are two ways of spreading light: to be
the candle or the mirror that reflects it.
— Edith Wharton

When we are going through a crisis or a time of emotional loss, sometimes the most difficult thing to do is to ask for help. That's exactly the time when we need the people in our lives to step up, reach out, and simply be there for us. At these times we need the person who reaches out to us to soothe, listen, and be compassionate.

The call came in the middle of the night. A close friend was killed by a drunk driver. No!!

It was nearly thirty years ago, but Sally remembers the phone call as if it were yesterday: a doctor who was a member of her temple was racing to the hospital ER to care for a patient in trauma when his car was broadsided by a drunk driver and he was killed instantly. He left behind a wife and six children.

"We were we were all devastated by the news," said Sally. "His funeral was on a Friday (and there was standing room only), and it occurred to me that after the initial impact and the outpouring of sympathy by the entire community, there would likely be a lull in the support that his wife would receive. That's not for lack of caring, but simply because people tend to extend themselves to those who are grieving closer to the time of death than afterward."

Words to Live By

"It was a chance to let her know that I hadn't forgotten that she was going through a terrible time and that I could provide a listening ear."

Sally had seen it happen several times and was determined to move in a different direction. The following Friday, a week after the funeral, she picked up her phone and called Pat, the doctor's widow.

"I just wanted to let her know I was thinking about her," said Sally.

The call became a weekly ritual. Every Friday, for more than a year, Sally called to express her concern and to remind Pat that she and the community around her were holding her family in their thoughts and prayers.

"It was a chance to let her know that I hadn't forgotten that she was going through a terrible time and that I could provide a listening ear," said Sally. "Sometimes our conversations were quite short; other times they lasted longer."

It wasn't until years later that Sally would learn how much the simple act of her calls helped to calm Pat's fears and bring peace into the chaos and emptiness of shattering loss.

"She told me how much she appreciated the calls and looked forward to them," said Sally. "Selfishly, it made me feel that I could do something, even though I couldn't change an awful situation."

Be the Solid and Calm One

"Without doing anything, things can sometimes go more smoothly just because of our peaceful presence. In a small boat when a storm comes, if one person remains solid and calm, others will not panic and the boat is more likely to stay afloat."
— Thich Nhat Hanh

Back in Action
An American Soldier's Story of Courage, Faith, and Fortitude

When David Rozelle crossed the finish line of the Coeur d'Alene Ironman in Idaho late in June of 2006, running, swimming, and biking alongside 2,200 professional athletes in the grueling race, he exemplified his personal life philosophy and served as a shining inspiration to others: "Never give up."

It was the first Ironman for the thirty-four-year-old army major, who is the first amputee to resume a dangerous command on the same battlefield.

In June 2003, less than two months after Rozelle and his troops crossed into Iraq, an antitank mine blew off his right foot. Rozelle fought through rehabilitation with gritty determination, using skiing and snowboarding as a part of his program. His athletic training later expanded to include triathlons and the New York Marathon, his recent Ironman, and leading an all military/all amputee triathlete team.

Refusing to let his injury stop him, Rozelle roared back into action, returning to Iraq as commander of an armored cavalry troop. These days he's back in the United States and serves as spokesperson for the Challenged Athlete's Foundation's Operation Rebound and at the Walter Reed Army Medical

Center in Washington, D.C., as administrator for the amputee care center. He is passionate and committed to his new mission: encouraging amputees by showing how he has made it.

At least 4,400 military men and women have been wounded in action since the United States invaded Afghanistan in 2001 and Iraq in 2003. Four hundred forty-eight of them have lost a limb. Some have lost two or three.

"These guys with no arms who have to go home and learn to live again? Shoot, I've got it easy," Rozelle says. "You talk to a guy that's missing both arms, and he'll look at you and say, 'Man, I'm sure glad I've got my legs.' You talk to a guy that's lost both his legs and he's (raising his arms) saying, 'I got these.'"

Rozelle recruits amputees to join him at sports clinics, ski races, and other events for disabled veterans.

"I sit in rooms with these guys who are crying and know that there's no one major bullet to help all of them," says Rozelle. "I try to make some kind of difference for each of them in their individual situations. And the best I can do is to try to help all of them find new goals for life deep inside themselves. I just try to help them have goals, again, to fight for something to live for."

Rozelle also is active with a number of charities including the Disabled Sports USA's Soldier's Fund and the HHS Campaign of the Presidential Physical Fitness Award for Children with Disabilities. He has been awarded the Bronze Star with Valor and the Purple Heart. In May, he and his wife Kim also welcomed their second son, Jackson.

When he's not at Walter Reed, always encouraging, always trying to reignite the spark inside, and sometimes just listening to the tears, he's testifying in Congress and training—one to four hours a day, five days a week, for his next Ironman.

"I'm a lucky, busy guy," says Rozelle. "I've got a lot of people here I can't stop fighting for."

Just Be Present

It is well to give when asked, but it is better to give unasked, through understanding.
—Kahlil Gibran

Just show up. That is what a friend once advised when a mutual friend was battling for his life in a hospital. Sometimes we don't realize how much it will mean to someone else if we do a simple thing, like showing up to say we care, even if it is just for a moment. Patrick Burke, a father of two and a human resources executive, learned that important lesson when he made the trek from his suburban Chicago home to his aunt's bedside at Rush Medical Center in Chicago. Patrick learned that just being there for someone helps repair that person's spirit. Maybe we all should ask ourselves, "Who needs us to show up at their side?"

When Patrick Burke learned his aunt Vera had cancer, he knew he had to do something. Like any large Irish family, Patrick's roster of first cousins and their spouses totaled at least a hundred people. Vera was one of eight aunts and uncles on his dad's side, his dad's oldest sister. Needless to say, with so many relatives, parades and parties—huge gatherings—were about as close as most of the Burke clan got.

"There's always a lot of talk flying around at family events, but very little 'real' connecting," Patrick is quick to point out. "And when there is real connecting, it's typically between the 'parents' and their siblings, my mom and dad interacting with the relatives in that generation, storytelling, sharing news about their kids, sharing worries about ill health, and that kind of thing.

"So, the fact that since I was a kid, I liked to hang out with the 'older generation,' made me somewhat of an oddity in the clan. I've always enjoyed 'real' conversations with whichever of my aunts or uncles would engage me. I'd enjoy talking politics or about life. It didn't happen all that often."

With his aunt Vera, it was an especially rare occurrence.

But, last year, when Vera was diagnosed with cancer, Patrick made it a priority to visit her in the hospital early in the journey.

"I just went to the hospital, one of her many nephews, and just sat with her," recalls Patrick. "To be honest it was a mix of sad, funny, and strange sitting there with my dad's older sister, whom I honestly didn't know that well and who honestly didn't know me so well.

"What was beautiful, however, is that this simple act of sitting, and visiting, as we Irish do, afforded me this chance to listen to my aunt, who was hurting, confused, alone, and afraid. She didn't cop to all of those feelings, but they were as present with her as her hospital gown," Patrick remembers.

"Like any Irish mother, she was fiercely proud of her family. She was trying to decide whether to join her daughter and family for the holidays, not wanting to burden them but also not wanting to be alone. We talked about it. We changed the subject. And, we talked about it again."

It was in the simple act of listening to his aunt and being fully present to the moment that Patrick says allowed him to do something he felt was meaningful and that helped her. He advised her—"in a very loving way"—to spend the holidays with her family. Best part: she listened and had a fabulous holiday.

Patrick and Vera spent almost two hours together, talking, laughing, and sharing relative stories. And, when he left, he got to do the most important thing, which he had never done before: "I got to tell her I love her."

Later, he would learn that his aunt Vera raved and raved to his parents about the visit from her "young"—forty-something— "dutiful" nephew.

Afterward, Patrick still believes it wasn't much that he did, except that he pushed himself to move beyond his own awkwardness and fear of hospitals to focus instead on the reality: he had a lonely, scared aunt who was very ill. "We'd never really had a one-on-one talk before, and illness opened the opportunity for us to do that. I decided to give her what I would have wanted in the same situation."

Words to Live By

"What was beautiful, however, is that this simple act of sitting, and visiting, as we Irish do, afforded me this chance to listen to my aunt, who was hurting, confused, alone, and afraid. She didn't cop to all of those feelings, but they were as present with her as her hospital gown."

Pumping Up Others with an Rx-for-Empathy Workout

The joy that compassion brings is one of the best-kept secrets of humanity. It is a secret known only to very few people, a secret that has to be rediscovered over and over again.
—Henri J. M. Nouwen

At seventy-seven years old, Konrad Bald knows one thing for sure: everything in his life has brought him to where he is. We may not always know what is calling us to action, but if we pay attention, the opportunities to help someone who is physically, mentally, or spiritually ailing are everywhere.

As a teenager growing up as one of four children living with their single mother in postwar Germany, Konrad had to beg for food. That is why he made a promise early on to help anyone and everyone, especially those suffering hunger.

And that's exactly what he's done. This retired human resources professional has dedicated his life to volunteering at hospitals, as a visitor for patients in behavioral health care facilities, shelters for the homeless, food pantries, and prisons.

When he's not "officially" cultivating compassion as a volunteer, he's creating compassionate interventions every waking minute. He smiles as he jests, "I've got eleven widows on my list." Joking aside, he and his wife Dell are the buffers against isolation and depression for nearly a dozen widows in their parish congregation and larger community of Barrington, Illinois. They gather with them several times a week for bridge, run errands, chauffeur to doctors' appointments, and sit bedside when illness has landed one of their elderly friends in the hospital.

What's more, every Monday, Wednesday, and Friday, from 4:30 to 9:00 A.M., Konrad Bald walks the line at the local YMCA. There, he has become an unofficial minister of care as he makes his way through the sweating masses, greeting everyone by name. The Y's longest standing part-time employee offers just the right words, spoken at the right moment, to challenge, comfort, and dare regulars into action.

We met Konrad a year ago and have been inspired and impressed by his consistent presence of support and shared wisdom for the Y regulars who daily share their health woes, concerns about ailing family members, and friendship for each other. He is at the center of a compassionate community he seems to have inspired, with regulars raising their hands to volunteer in his multitude of caring endeavors. He's a role model for the belief that compassion can be a pathway to better health and happiness.

His actions inspire. Whenever Konrad spots a pregnant woman; he tells her he is saying a prayer for her. (His daughter lost a child through a miscarriage and he knows the pain.) When Brody, an elderly blind fellow and regular at the Y, marches in the door with his cane, Konrad is immediately is at his side, escorting him for the next half-hour from machine to machine, and jesting, "I've got ya next to a really pretty lady today." For others, it is advice: "He who rests, rusts."

"He's a gentle man, with an open heart who is compassionate and committed to helping everyone," says Pat Harrington, director of the homeless shelters in Chicago's northwest suburbs.

Carrying Each Other: Konrad's Lessons from Along the Way

On what it takes to care: "You have to have empathy, to really be able to put yourself in someone else's shoes and feel how they feel."

On getting started: "You have to listen. I learned in a hospital ministry that your job is to listen."

On opening up: "You need to prove you can be trusted before people will open up to let you help them."

On small acts: "Caring is all about just being there to let someone talk. You reach out, you let them know you care, and then you let them tell you their story."

On never giving up: Konrad spent his high school benched with a heart murmur, staring outside at the kids playing soccer. Later in the army, doctors said it was a mistake. He had been born six weeks premature, and his grandmother had her funeral dress sewn at the birth, anticipating he would not make it. "Cherish every day. There is never enough time."

On fate and giving back: "I knew starvation and pledged that I would do whatever I could to help those who hunger."

On love and laughter: Ask Konrad about his wife Dell, who works out alongside him at the Y and cooks for the homeless shelter, about his recipe for love. He fell in love with her at first sight, during his first week at Cornell University. As of 2:00 P.M. Eastern Time on a recent day in April, he tells you they have been married fifty-three years, nine months, and seven days. "Every day counts," he says.

The Write Stuff

By Mary Beth Sammons

Sometimes what we choose to do does not matter nearly as much as the fact that we choose to do something. That we choose to demonstrate our love and concern for one another, for example, is often more important than how we choose to express it. The memory that we cared may in fact be all that endures.

—Frederick W. Schmidt, *What God Wants for Your Life*

Words can have a powerful impact. They can bring us such insight and inspiration. Many of us have found that in some of our toughest crises or during our greatest losses, someone offers just the right words and insight that make all the difference. This is what happened when one high school boy, my son Thomas, found out that one of his best friends had been rushed to the hospital that afternoon. His friend was lying nearly paralyzed from the neck down with Guillain-Barre Syndrome.

Our sixteen-year-old neighbor, Matt, had been rushed to the hospital after collapsing on his bedroom floor. Hours later we would learn he had a rare condition that could leave him weak and paralyzed for a long, long time.

Without asking or telling anyone, my son Thomas, then a sophomore in high school, rediscovered a blank journal I had once given him as "a safe place to share his feelings" (to which, at the time of gifting, he responded by looking at me, rolling his eyes, and throwing it in his drawer untouched. Intention: never to touch again).

Finding Mr. Good Inside of You

In J. R. R. Tolkien's *The Hobbit,* Thorin says to Bilbo, "There is more in you of good than you know . . . some courage and some wisdom blended in measure." Sometimes it is only when someone we love or care for very much faces crisis, illness, or loss that we realize that inside us we have something powerful to give. The challenge is to have the courage to find it, and not to be frightened to reach inside so we can share the simple virtues of friendship and compassion with someone who needs us.

Questions to Help You Find the Ways to Say, "I Care, You Are Not Alone"

Illness robs us of the daily rituals, everyday moments that connect us to our lives and to the people that we love the most. Losing these connections can be frustrating, stressful, and very disappointing. To care, to reach out, here are some questions we might ask ourselves:

+ How can we become a gift during someone's trying times?
+ What can we do to provide support in their illness?
+ Should we bring over a casserole?
+ What about recording a laughter tape or their favorite music?
+ Is there something tangible we can do to say we care, such as writing inspirational thoughts or motivating quotes?
+ Have inspirational books helped me through hard times? Maybe it is time to share them with someone else.

Words to Live By
"I didn't know what else to do."

But on this day, he retrieved the empty journal, headed down the block to the high school, and went gym to gym, practice field to practice field, getting teammates on the volleyball team, cheerleaders, teachers, and coaches—anyone he could find to write words of inspiration to his best buddy, Matt. On the first two pages, he—my son, who does not ever write—wrote a moving tribute to the friend he'd known since he was two.

Scared to death after seeing the paramedics haul his friend away the day before, he found the courage to go to the hospital on his own—"No, Mom, I don't need you to go with me. I can go alone"—with his book in hand. "I didn't know what else to do," he later said.

For the next month, Thomas became one of Matt's bedside regulars. I'm not sure what kind of impact the maroon journal and the well-wishes had on Matt, but Thomas's mother Mary knows that the actions of her son left an indelible mark on her heart. "If anyone learned anything that day from the journal entries, it was me. I learned that no matter what, if we search our hearts, we might come up with something that we can do to help or inspire someone else, something that might surprise and inspire ourselves, mostly."

Getting Started: The Inside Track on Carrying Each Other

Stop! That is what happens at the moment the call comes in. Your world *stops!* It's a moment that will change your life. One of life's great paradoxes is that it sometimes takes a brush with illness or loss for us to see what really matters. And, at these times, we are called on to make choices to reach out and care, choices that we may not have made had there not been an urgency created by the crisis at hand. These moments can be wake-up calls, giving us the opportunity to trust ourselves more and move in grace to reach out to another.

♥ From the CarePages Frontlines

Doing a Little Shopping

"After my mom's mastectomy (two-time, now twelve-year survivor), I went to a local department store and bought all the tops/dresses from the clearance rack in her size with buttons down the front, no stripes, no words across the chest, etc., and brought them home. My Mom appreciated being able to try on things in the privacy of her home, then I returned what she didn't like or didn't fit! I'll always remember that shopping trip."
— Caitlin Anderson

Making Peace through Writing

"My mom lost her ten-month battle with inflammatory breast cancer in 2005. My sister and I were at my mom's side all the time, as it was very frightening for her and she was always sick with the chemo. Sometimes she had a hard time expressing her thoughts and feelings. So we kept a daily journal of her thoughts and feelings and what she was most thankful for that day. Sometimes the person is afraid to discuss out loud with their loved ones how they feel. It helps to write it all down."
— Chris Agricola

CHAPTER 3

LETTING GO

We Can't Change This or Make It Different,
but We Can Move through This by Giving
Our All to an Ailing Loved One

*Diseases can be our spiritual flat tires—disruptions
in our lives that seem to be disastrous at the time but
end by redirecting our lives in a meaningful way.*
—Bernie Siegel

If we are honest with ourselves, most of us have difficulty in
dealing with our own feelings when a friend or loved one is
diagnosed with a life-changing or life-threatening illness. The
news of illness catalyzes a rush of conflicting emotions—fear,

grief, anger, panic, and sometimes shame that we don't know exactly what to do or say when confronted with this bad news. We can also feel afraid or inadequate. We might believe that we just don't have it within ourselves to care for someone whose illness or disability forces us to confront the fact that it's not a perfect world.

Sometimes we find ourselves tossing out the well-worn phrase, "If there is anything I can do, just call." We find ourselves desperately looking for words and actions that are comfortable beyond "I'm sorry." Or at other times, we find ourselves so uncertain of what to do or say, we stop calling. We disappear.

We may want to offer help, but we don't know what to do. It is exactly at that point that we need to face our own fears and emotional fragility and accept that is okay for us to be upset.

We don't have to fix the person. But we can look to illness or permanent disability as a place of grace, where we can invite our friend or loved one to help us help him or her. By being there in whatever way we most comfortably can, we open ourselves to the spiritual promises of healing and hope that are calling on us to treasure each single day. We may not do it all right, but by moving through our own fears, we open ourselves to the potential for closeness with another, the potential to heal hurts and make connections before it is too late.

In his book *Anam Cara* ("Soul Friend"), Irish writer John O'Donohue talks about how real friends (or family who are there for us) are the people who show up exactly at those moments when someone is having a rough time and needs *you*— needs a friend.

These friends and family are the people who have learned how to reach inside themselves to be there during life's toughest challenges. O'Donohue says, "If you look back along your life, you will see that at the crucial thresholds, different people were sent to you to help you acknowledge what was going on, to recognize your own responsibility, and to bring you over thresholds."

Here, we are inspired by the stories of a sister, family members, and even a stranger who found ways to respond with sincerity and kindness during times of suffering.

We Are Family

In Saying Good-bye, They Found a Way to Keep a Sister's Funny, Joyous Spirit Adventuring

An aged man is but a paltry thing,
A tattered coat upon a stick, unless
Soul clap its hands and sing, and louder sing
For every tatter in its mortal dress,
Nor is there singing school but studying
Monuments of its own magnificence;
And therefore I have sailed the seas and come
To the holy city of Byzantium.
—William Butler Yeats, "Sailing to Byzantium"

With or without you is the feeling we find ourselves facing when death is knocking at the door of a loved one. When the call came that her sister was very ill, Mavis Hawley DeWees found that everything that had mattered to her was overthrown. Suddenly, nothing was more important than getting across the country to her sister's side. Even though by day Mavis is a psychotherapist and guides dozens of patients, she had no protocol to help her deal with the fact that her sister was facing a powerful enemy that would soon take her life. Knowing her sister was going to die and striving to keep her spirit alive—during the downslide and forever—became critical for Mavis, not only for her sister's memory, but for her own emotional survival.

On Loss

In some ways, what we went through helped us gain greater compassion for others who were struggling or dealing with so much tragedy. Ours was so public, and at one point, I could have sent in a checklist for my sons' school ticking off the reasons they weren't there: My uncle Chris died, my grandma died, my aunt was diagnosed with cancer, my grandpa had a stroke at Thanksgiving, my aunt died.

But crisis living teaches you survival in a different light. The moment you are diagnosed with cancer, you become a survivor living in the moment. We had to look at it like, my sister is still here, other people go through this. Okay, what can we do? Dana and Chris both decided to create a positive legacy. They wanted to leave a legacy of living every moment until the last second.

—Deborah Morosini, M.D., sister of Dana Reeve, and sister-in-law of Christopher Reeve, and spokesperson for The Bonnie J. Addario Lung Cancer Foundation

Naomi Brown liked to live where her vibrant spirit and creative energy led her—Barcelona, Spain; New York City; Mexico; Switzerland; California; and finally Cabbagetown in Atlanta, Georgia.

An eclectic thinker, painter, historian, fighter of injustice, and consultant to costumers for filmmakers, the headline on her obituary in the *Atlanta Journal-Constitution* proclaimed, "Naomi Brown marched to the beat of a different drummer." After all, she was a percussionist who played drums in high school in the 1950s when girls simply weren't playing drums in marching bands. In the '60s she was drumming for jazz combos when women weren't doing that either. She threw parties where Bob Dylan and Buffy St. Marie would jam and ushered at the Atlanta Symphony Orchestra. She was raised by a mother named Myrtice and left behind three daughters, four grandchildren, and a group of friends she had been collecting all her life—which ended on July 18, 2004. When she started feeling ill, she was diagnosed with irritable bowel syndrome. By the time she sought serious medical attention, she was too sick to recover, and she died of peritoneal cancer.

In her final months at the hospital, and the last day's bedside at her home in Atlanta, her huge support network of friends, her boss, Pam, and her family took turns holding her hands. Her sister, Mavis Hawley DeWees, a psychotherapist, and Mavis's partner, Carole Hines, traveled frequently back and forth from San Francisco. They sent an airline ticket to Mavis's daughter so that she could fly from Montana to say good-bye to her idol, "Aunt Naomi."

For a brief respite, Naomi started feeling better, and Mavis promised her she would take her anywhere in the world she wanted to go. The trio adventured around the globe to Turkey and Greece. "She had a blast," Mavis remembers. "I will never forget her taking out a folded piece of paper one night in Istanbul. She read Yeats's 'Sailing to Byzantium' to me."

Later, Mavis and Carole had made arrangements to meet Naomi in New York City to see the *Glories of Byzantium* show at the Met. But Naomi had a major setback and the trip was cancelled.

In the last weeks, Mavis flew to Atlanta as much as possible to be with Naomi.

The sadness hung heavy in the final days when Mavis watched her sister disappearing before her eyes. She experienced an almost desperate need to be close to her. They had never been a touchy-feely family. But now her sister needed her to lie beside her and hold her.

Says Mavis, "Her house was small, really small. Her bedroom contained the two of us. But slowly it became our room as we started to trust each other, and I realized my sister was going to leave. We stayed up at night because this was the worst time for pain, the pain of loss, I suspect.

"We talked about nothing, really. Her garden that needed care, dahlias lifting their heads to the moon, the birds. How could they live in a neighborhood where trees were so quickly disappearing at the hands of callous builders? We talked about her two big dogs. Who would take her twelve-year-old Paddy who was blind and deaf and unable to jump up on the bed? She finally got it. And we stayed always at home. I hung on to the sister who would forever remain as always my leader. My teacher. The boss.

"I loved her with an urgency, knowing I would never see her again. She hugged me. At the end, it was hard to realize that despite all the time I had spent 'breathing her' back to life so that she would stay with me, I couldn't go where she was going," recalls Mavis.

The last time Naomi was in the hospital, Carole, too, stayed with Naomi in her room "and just gave her some company, bought her a nice nightgown, and listened to music with her."

Friends, ex-husbands, and all who loved Naomi gathered to eulogize her in Atlanta's Piedmont Park, grieved, and went home. Naomi had written her own speech, which was read by her boss and friend, Pam. A bagpiper played "Abide with Me." There were also a cellist and a fiddler, and one neighbor brought a box with frogs in it. She set them free in the lake in the park. Everyone gave a speech, and they played Tallulah Bankhead's "I'll Be Seeing You." They floated her ashes in little magnolia leaf boats at sundown.

The good-bye ritual was vintage Naomi. Police approached funeral goers, concerned about some of the photos posted on park property. The police were nice and left the celebrants alone. But, Naomi's daughter Jeannie Cooper was quick to point out, "Mom always said that it wasn't really a party unless the cops showed up."

Solace for Mavis and Carole to this day comes in the memories of Naomi's larger-than-life presence, her memory, and in staying in touch with Naomi's friends in Atlanta and all over the globe.

Words to Live By

"I loved her with an urgency, knowing I would never see her again. She hugged me. At the end, it was hard to realize that despite all the time I had spent 'breathing her' back to life so that she would stay with me, I couldn't go where she was going."

"She was the strongest woman I have ever known, and she had the bearing of a soldier," says Mavis. "She never sagged, no matter how much pain she was in. She had many young friends, and she was always the last one to want to go home."

Last year, to commemorate the first anniversary of Naomi's passing, they got together with some of Naomi's friends for martinis at the Algonquin Hotel in New York, where they had planned to take Naomi if she had made it to the Byzantium show. Naomi had picked outfits for them all to wear.

This year friends and family gathered to toast Naomi's birthday with cake and champagne.

"Mostly, she is just with us—in our thoughts—all the time," says Carole. "But it is also becoming possible now to think of doing something more formal, making a contribution to the Atlanta Symphony or something like that. It has just been really hard."

Tips for Caring for a Dying Sister

Go for it. Jump into the adventure and journey of dying with your friend or family member.

Lean on me. Become that person's partner. Be in cahoots with whatever they need or want.

Practice self-compassion. Be sure to take care of yourself, and try to remain strong.

Be the hope. Your loved one counts on you to walk beside him or her and to lend your support. But they need to feel that you will go on living your own life.

Love with heartstrings. Detach with love from their pain.

That's the way they like it. Let them do what they need to do. Respect their right to live and die the way they want to.

Be the protector. Protect dying people from well-meaning individuals who turn them into objects of pity.

Create beauty. Help the dying person by helping him maintain his appearance, her paint her nails.

Savor the music. Listen with them to the music they love.

Keep it simple. Do whatever it takes to create comfort and dignity for your loved one. If he wants to see friends, welcome them. If she can't answer another phone call, let the machine answer the phone.

Provide a healing touch. Touch them often. Stay close.

Too Soon for Long Good-byes

A Daughter Struggles to Stay in the Moment as She Watches the Long, Slow Fade of Her Parents to Alzheimer's
By Laurie Borman

Our limitations serve, our wounds serve,
even our darkness can serve.
—Rachel Naomi Remen

When doctors confirmed that both her parents had Alzheimer's disease, the hardest part was not planning too far ahead or trying too hard to recapture the past. In the following story, Highwood, Illinois, writer Laurie Borman, a mother of two sons, chronicles in her own words her struggle to care for her own children, work full-time, and carry both her elderly parents through this heartbreaking diagnosis. She is grateful for the team effort shared by her sister Julianne and her brother Scott.

Alzheimer's disease is called a long good-bye because people with it fade into death, slowly, inevitably. First there is the forgetting. When my dad, a materials engineer, couldn't tell me what type of paint to use on my front door, I knew something was wrong. It took two years of coaxing my mother to get him to a neurologist. I suspected she didn't want to confirm what we already knew. Medication would only slow the progress of his Alzheimer's.

Years ago, after reading Dr. Sherwin B. Nuland's book, *How We Die*, I was thinking that Alzheimer's was the worst way to die. Dad would not survive, and how could we? My mom seemed to be sticking her head in the sand, ignoring Dad's needs. Soon my sister, brother, and I discovered that Mom, too, had Alzheimer's.

While there's no easy way to deal with the illness, I found that it helped not to plan too far ahead or try too hard to recapture the past. It was best to stay in the moment, reaching out to my parents just where they were.

Initially, my parents stayed in their own home. We hired a cleaning service, since my mom also had macular degeneration, causing blindness in one eye and making it difficult for her to see how dirty the house was. They gave up living in Florida for the winter, and that brought on feelings of isolation because my dad could no longer drive. We found a wonderful adult day care facility for Alzheimer's patients, and Dad went three days a week. We also found an adult care service that could take Dad and Mom out to local shops, museums, and other excursions.

I took vacation days each year with them, driving to visit Indiana's Amish country, sampling kettle corn and shoo-fly pie. They could still enjoy a good meal. We met with their financial advisor and went to all their banks, adding my name to the accounts "just for emergencies." Until that day, I had never been permitted any knowledge of my parents' finances. We found that my dad liked getting my monthly reports of their financials, set in large-print type and simplified with just a few accounts. We hired an elder-law attorney to draw up a new will for them, along with a living will. It was one of the last times my dad was able to sign his name.

Slowly, Dad withdrew. He had great difficulty finding the right words for what he wanted to say. I knew he liked to get out, so we'd walk slowly around the block. I'd take him and my mom to the store, but it was like having two toddlers wandering in different directions and at different speeds.

Eventually their house got to be too much. My sister was cleaning the pool for them; a chore my dad once relished and now could not remember how to do. My mom forgot to make meals, and my dad was unable to make things for himself. My siblings and I feared they might leave the stove on or let a stranger in the house. An infestation of drain flies due to a water leak under the house was our excuse to get them to sample assisted living facilities.

We found a place near my parents' and my sister's house. It was a new facility, with big porches all around the outside and an elegant dining room serving three meals a day. They would have their own apartment. Reluctantly, my parents packed their bags. For weeks my mom would call from the assisted living home in a panic, wondering why they were in a hotel and when they were going home. My dad would wink at us when he said they'd packed their bags because Mom thought they were going home that day. He knew they weren't going back, but my mom couldn't bear the thought of leaving their home.

They once loved to travel, but since that was no longer possible, my sister, brother, and I would take them to a local pub that featured Irish bands. My dad enjoyed just listening to the music, and maybe having a sip of Guinness. We'd order meals for him—he couldn't articulate what he wanted—getting food that didn't spill easily.

In April 2005, Dad found he couldn't walk at all without pain. He insisted he have knee replacement surgery. Little did we know this would be the real beginning of the end. He was a different person after the surgery, striking out at nurses and not opening his eyes. He was moved from the hospital to the assisted living facility's nursing home section. Slowly the physical therapist got my dad to get up and walk a short distance without assistance.

We tried to live in the moment with him, visiting his room, bringing photos that he might recognize, and our small dog. He grew up on a farm and loved animals. He rallied for a while, but he seemed upset when he recognized that he was in a nursing home. We encouraged my mom to put lotion on his hands. We gave him haircuts in his room. He introduced my son as his son-in-law to the nursing staff. A few weeks later, he'd begun to decline again. After my visit, he told me to "come and see me again sometime" as if I were a complete stranger. He never spoke to me again after that.

We hired a medical van to bring my dad home one last time that summer. My brother built a ramp to the front door so he could be wheeled in. He sat on the screen porch, gazing out at the pool. My sister fed him a hot dog from the grill.

Each visit, he declined a bit more. I just tried to do whatever he was capable of enjoying, dancing with him in his wheelchair to the tunes of the Lawrence Welk show. He seemed to enjoy the music. We had a CD player in his room, and brought the dog in to pet. The time came when he couldn't pet the dog, though.

At Thanksgiving, we brought his favorite pies and my sister fed him a bit of each. The grandkids ran around the halls as we chatted.

When the nursing staff suggested hospice care in mid-December, I came and stayed. I brought a laptop, checked e-mails from his room, pointed out the birds outside, and just carried on a one-way conversation. My sister and brother visited daily, along with my mom.

On December 23, my dad opened his eyes and looked at my brother, my sister, my mother, and me, sitting in his room. He didn't really seem to recognize any of us, but we were so grateful to see his blue eyes one last time. Then he closed his eyes and seemed to want to sleep. He hadn't eaten anything for a few days, and attempts to give him food only resulted in his prolonged coughing.

Earlier that day, my mother had fallen in her room. The ice on her ankle didn't keep the swelling down, so my sister and brother took her to the emergency room while I stayed with my dad, holding his hand as he slept. It was a quiet, peaceful afternoon.

The next morning, my sister and I arrived at his room to find him curled up, fighting for every breath. We tried to adjust him, but no position helped. Looking up, I saw birds at the bird feeder outside his window. "Look, Dad, the birds are back!" I said. When I looked over, his wracked breathing slowed. My sister and I held him and stroked his arms. In the end, touch was what we could give.

Words to Live By
"My sister and I held him and stroked his arms. In the end, touch was what we could give."

My father, Marion E. Denning, died the morning of Christmas Eve 2005. My mother still doesn't think she attended his funeral. While cleaning out their house, my sister found a year's worth of letters my parents wrote while Dad was stationed in Korea. Mom reads and rereads them. We just accept her where she is, and live in the moment. It's all we have.

Giving Her All to Her Ailing Son
Parents of Seriously Ill or Disabled Children Called on 24/7 to Care

Hope is a choice.
—Dallas Physician and cancer survivor
   Wendy Schlessel Harpham

Many parents of seriously ill or injured youth must pick up and care for their medically fragile children in their living rooms. The decision to be there 24/7 is one many parents don't regret. Yet, it is a life they never thought would be so difficult. When Becky Lawson-Ross's son Cody was nearly killed in an automobile accident and left paralyzed, she became his 'round-the-clock Florence Nightingale.

When she said good-bye to her son Cody after the family party she threw at her Rockford, Illinois, home for his fifteenth birthday, Becky Lawson-Ross says she had no idea it would be the last time she would see him as "a normal teen." "Cody insisted he wanted to go out," the thirty-eight-year-old Becky remembers. "I had a gut feeling to say no, but I let him."

At 2:30 A.M. the phone rang. All Becky could hear was crying. The call was from Jessica, a girl who was in the car with Cody and the others. "My world fell apart," recalls Becky. "Jessica was sobbing and telling me Cody and Jason (his older stepbrother) were in an accident. The firemen were still trying to get Cody out of the car."

The next call Becky made was to the police.

"I didn't know what to do. I called the police station and told them the information I received. They did not tell me too much. They verified that, yes, there was a car accident, and the patient was taken to the hospital."

And the police told Becky to get to the hospital, immediately.

On the way from her rural home, she stopped to pick up her mother, sensing in her gut that something was really wrong. En route to the hospital, they spotted the smoldering remains of a recent accident, stopped and watched as the stunned police and paramedics stared with disbelief into their eyes, muttering the mantra, "You better get to the hospital."

The police and paramedics knew what had happened. Becky still didn't.

Arriving at Rockford Memorial Hospital, Becky raced to the ER. Doctors told her to wait outside.

Finally, a doctor emerged. It was not good news. Cody's body was mangled, and he was losing blood as fast as they could funnel it into his body. His pelvis was crushed, his arteries torn. He was off to surgery to try to stop the internal bleeding. Most of his bones were broken, his right femur, right foot, and pelvis shattered, right hand broken in five places, and his left ankle and wrist also broken.

The doctors told Becky that Cody's chance for survival was less than 50 percent.

"They also told me his heart had been under so much strain that it could stop beating at any time," she recalls. "I was at a loss. I was in shock."

A year later, she has a blurry memory of some people waiting with her and her mother during the time Cody was in surgery. She says, "I just wanted to curl up and not talk to anybody. I remember somebody making me take a few bites of food. How could I eat when my son was fighting for his life? Finally around 8:00 P.M. Cody was moved to the pediatric ICU at the University of Wisconsin in Madison. The doctors warned us that we might not recognize him, that he had started to swell and was attached to a lot of tubes and machines." They told her Cody was the worst trauma patient the hospital had ever treated.

"He really didn't look as bad as I expected. Yes, he looked really bad, but I was prepared for the worst."

Becky now reflects, "Who was to know that the worst was yet to come?"

"It was hard for me to see him like that. I had to leave the room," says Becky. "I didn't want him to hear me cry. I know now he would not have."

For months, Cody was tethered to life support.

Becky says she doesn't see the strength in herself. But her determination speaks volumes, not only in words but in actions. "I am a mother, and I was going to do whatever it took to keep my son alive."

And she did. She lived at the hospital, sleeping on a cot beside his bed. She quit her job of eleven years, repairing two-way radios at Motorola, to become her son's sole around-the-clock caregiver. She remembers little things that pulled her through, like a resident coming over one morning and wrapping his arms around her, telling her she looked like she needed a big hug. On one particularly bad day, when hope seemed dim, the trauma coordinator took Becky to lunch in the cafeteria to make sure she was eating and to lend a consoling ear and a boost of encouragement.

Becky rarely complains, but says she owes a lot of thanks to her mom for the occasional breaks.

"People who have not been in this situation do not realize how isolated it can make you feel," says Becky in a rare moment of reflection. "Before, I had all of my coworkers to talk to every day, and I got to see other people. For so long after the accident I never left the house. I couldn't leave Cody. Our only link to the outside community was CarePages and our online community."

A year after the accident, Becky says her life has changed completely from the day, March 5, 2006, when the car Cody's friend was driving hit a tree at 70 mph. It was a month before anyone knew if Cody would live. His mom says it is a "miracle" he survived.

The good news is there are signs of hope. In summer 2006, a year after the accident, Cody stood for several seconds with the help of a therapy belt and his occupational therapist. He also wiggled his toes. A tutor teaches Cody at home so he can finish his freshman and sophomore high school studies and move on to his junior year. For most of the first year, books replaced the friends that were once always there and now connect mostly through e-mails. "I think it is hard for other kids to see their friend like this," says Becky. "Cody understands; he just knows that everything from here on is up to him and he needs to operate day by day. He's determined to walk again."

Cody is one of the legions of teens who have been injured or left paralyzed in an automobile accident—more than 300,000 a year nationwide. Others are struck down by chronic illness or disease, facing difficult challenges that sometimes leave them sad, angry, and scared as they wait for cures that might not exist or hope to someday walk again.

For their caregivers, it can be a particularly tough challenge. Everyone's lives have changed, and they must struggle to find a new way.

Cody and Becky are learning these lessons the hard way.

"We don't look at what went away," says Becky. "We look at how lucky we are that Cody is alive. There is still a lot of hope that he might walk again. He finally was able to wiggle his toe on his left foot for the first time a couple of weeks ago. Better days will come."

As a result of the "great compassion and care Cody received during his stay at University of Wisconsin hospital," Becky decided to switch careers and go to school to become a nurse to work in a Pediatric Intensive Care Unit. She started her first classes in the nursing program in August 2006. "I only hope that by doing this I can give back what we received to some other person," says Becky.

Words to Live By
"I am a mother, and I was going to do whatever it took to keep my son alive."

Tips for Parents Who Are the Heart and Soul of Their Teen's Illness and Suffering

Battling disease or suffering the aftermath of a horrible accident is grueling at any age, but it can be particularly tough on teens. It's a situation once-active teens like Cody never would have imagined.

Adolescence alone is a stressful developmental process even for physically healthy teens. Here are some tips to help parents cope with caring for a teen:

Be kind to yourself. For parents, seeing their child paralyzed or ill is a profoundly crushing blow and brings out the parental instinct to hover—just what the teens don't want, says Char Wenc, a nationally recognized speaker, author on parenting, and professor in the doctoral programs at the Adler School of Professional Psychology and Loyola University in Chicago.

Promote independence. "Illness or injury takes away what is most important to teens—their independence," says Wenc, a mother of two grown boys. "They want more than ever to belong to the peer group and to break away from their parents, not to mention how concerned they are about their physical appearance. Being in a hospital or a wheelchair puts them under a magnifying glass and sabotages their independence."

Be creative about connecting. Despite the push-pull to be independent, teens do need to connect with their parents and with those who support them more than ever during illness, says LeAnn Thieman, coauthor of *Chicken Soup for the Caregiver's Soul.* "I often remind grown-ups, mostly parents, that we need to talk to and give attention to our teens whether they seem to want it or not. Even though they roll their eyes, or simply grunt a response, or leave the room, what I know is, deep down they are glad we show them we care."

Be sensitive to the fear. "The problem with having a sick friend is that it is very scary, so teens might stay away from the hospital or friend in a wheelchair because they don't know what to do or say," says Wenc. "This is especially devastating for the ill teen, who then feels completely abandoned."

Step in. It's up to parents to step in and actively recruit visitors and teen friends to their child's bedside, stresses Wenc.

From the CarePages Frontlines

Be There to Listen

"When my sister was diagnosed with breast cancer I was in a state of shock. You never think about it hitting so close to home. But in an instant, everything changes—for the person who is diagnosed mostly and for family and close friends. I learned that whatever you do after their surgery is everything. Don't ask. Just do. Think about what they would be doing if they were not in bed recuperating . . . laundry, dishes, walking the dog, feeding the pets, picking up around the house, watering plants, and anything else. Try to think like they think. Most of all be there to listen. Don't be pushy, and the best tip I saw on the message page was leaving a cooler at the front door. Sometimes

you don't feel like talking and having someone looking at you. Remember, breast cancer patients get very tired. Good news. My sister is a five-year survivor and she still loves to shop, so I know she is going to be okay!"
—*Martha Kellogg*

CHAPTER 4

CONNECTION

Finding the Openings to Help One Another

When something enters your life that is so big and as
non-negotiable as catastrophic illness, you either go in
denial for a while . . . or ultimately you accept it and you
make space for it. And in making space for it, you illuminate
a lot of things that you normally don't have room for . . .
you simply just look at the world differently.
—Michael J. Fox

What do you say? What do you do when someone you love or care
deeply about needs your help? What do you do when you want to
provide comfort and be present for a loved one who is facing

illness or loss? One of the most difficult things that sick and dis-abled people encounter is the discomfort that many well and able-bodied people feel in the face of infirmity. One can feel uncomfortable with people who are disfigured or disabled and get nervous and worry about saying or doing the wrong thing.

There are no right or wrong answers. But pay attention, because we have learned over and over again that the person who is experiencing the time of sorrow will give us signs that dare us into action. Sometimes when our fiercely independent friends say, "I'm okay," what they really mean is, "Don't let my outside fool you. I'm not as brave and strong as I seem. Ignore my protests that I can do this all myself. I can't," explains Bonnie Addario, a lung cancer survivor who realized early on in her diagnosis that the way through her battle was to let others in to help.

The only thing we have learned for certain is that illness and loss take away all control. You can't take away someone's illness. You cannot bring back the person who died. But you can reach out and help someone who's in inconsolable grief or is going through tough times. You just do. You do what you have to do to get through.

That is the resounding mantra we hear again and again from the people who write to us through *CarePages.com.* They tell us they are clinging like a lifeline to the friends and family who are there for them, that inside they cry, "Stay with me! Stay with me through this." And, the most comforting words someone can say to them: "I care about you. I am here."

We have witnessed the armies of people who have stepped out of their own comfort to do exactly that: to carry the load for someone else with compassion and caring during that person's greatest pain and sorrow.

For whatever reason, suffering—physical, emotional, or spiri-tual—opens us up to a whole new dimension of care and character. Many lessons can be learned through our collective woundedness and the indomitable will to live with courage and strength no matter what life throws in our path.

Here, we share the journeys of some who have faced the emotional, spiritual, and physical challenge of disease and life-threatening illness and the friends and loved ones who have moved to their sides. At some levels, it is difficult to understand the "whys." But perhaps it is through the mystery of those questions that we can tap into the wisdom of healing.

The lessons will be interpreted differently by each of us. It is our challenge to humbly soak them in and search within ourselves for the best way to move forward with compassion and caring.

Our intention is to present the raw realities and, we hope, to learn from them. We listened to the lived experience of those who have been challenged by serious illness and those who are trying to support them. Every person responded in ways more compelling than the cancer, chronic illness, or suffering they were going through.

Let Them Lead the Way
Alive with Passion and the Will to Survive, This Super-Achiever Took the Lead in Showing Others How to Care for Her

Never doubt that a small group of thoughtful committed citizens can change the world; indeed, it is the only thing that ever has.
—Margaret Mead

In the beginning, Bonnie Addario reacted to her diagnosis of lung cancer with terror. Two things stand out from the hazy curtain that hung over most of the first few days. One is that she refused to view the illness as a death sentence; there was a lot she could do to fight it. The second was her fear for her three children—her daughters Danielle and Andrea and her son Jared—then young adults, and their new families: her sons-in-law and her grandchildren. She realized they needed her now more than ever. The thought that cancer could rob her of her future with them was tormenting.

Fifty-five years old at the time of her diagnosis, Bonnie was matter-of-fact, strong, and always grounded. She was the kind of person who takes care of everyone else. Seldom sick before this, Bonnie was not accustomed to operating at less than full strength. She had no experience in letting others help her.

"I was terrified, but I thought I had to put up a strong front," recalls the San Carlos, California, resident. "I cried in the shower."

Bonnie began chemotherapy in mid-December 2003 and started brushing out handfuls of her hair around Christmas.

There was no instruction book on how to cope, how to let others in. All she knew was that she was filled with fear and heartbroken because her grandchildren were so afraid of her new less-than-perfect look.

She decided to use humor.

On Christmas night, as the family gathered at their winter home in Tahoe, she and her daughters marched up the stairs, drew funny symbols on her head with the razor, and when it was complete, they marched downstairs to show her son, son-in-law, and her husband Tony.

"I didn't want to spend one more day deflecting these taboo subjects," recalls Bonnie. "I was determined. We were going to learn to laugh at this and make the most of it. And we did. So, there was my smooth, bare head, and that was that."

It wasn't that the cancer was a secret. Everyone knew. But Bonnie struggled to keep the rhythms of her routine and instructed her husband Tony to make all the calls. Letters, stacks of them from friends, family, and coworkers at the petroleum company where she was the head honcho, piled up on the family's dining room table. She left them unopened for months.

This all worked pretty well, except that Bonnie learned that cancer "is a very lonely disease."

She remembers one day in particular.

"I was sitting on the BarcaLounger at the hospital outpatient clinic, with the chemo drip, wanting to puke and telling myself, 'Remember you are strong, you can do this.' Then I looked across the room and saw this woman about my age, and another woman, I think it was her mother, just sitting next to her, holding her hand and a Thermos for her to drink from. I was alone. And that is when I felt the loneliness like a blow. I realized I needed to learn to tell the people around me I needed them."

The challenge for Bonnie: to learn how to receive help with dignity and not lessen her sense of worth.

"My family was there steadfastly, even though they were very afraid," says Bonnie. "My husband was a rock and never made me feel like I was the disease. He took me to doctors' appointments, radiation treatments, and chemo all the time. You never really know just who you are married to until you need them. My children were also there for me. We didn't talk much about it, but I am sure they had a great deal to say to their extended families and friends."

On the friend front, Bonnie says it was easier for them to talk to Tony or her children to see how she was doing rather than talk directly to her. This seemed to work best.

"Just knowing that they were following my progress, checking on me, sending cards and flowers made my days easier," she says. "But for unknown reasons, I didn't open any of the cards until I was on my way to recovery. I couldn't bring myself to do it. They just kept piling up. When I did open them, I cried and cried. Some of the tears were for relief, but most were for the kind words and the love I felt reading the words, which I will cherish forever. I have saved each and every one of them."

In March, it will be three years since Bonnie was diagnosed with lung cancer. It has been a long road, with surgery after surgery. Through cancer, she discovered an indomitable will to live, courage to open up to other people's compassion, and the ability to heal over and over again. Visit the foundation she launched, the Bonnie J. Addario Lung Cancer Foundation, at *www.abreathawayfromthecure.org.*

Tips from Bonnie on How to Care for a Friend

As someone who has been there, Bonnie Addario knows there is a lot you can do to help a friend through the hard times of illness. Here's her list of simple things that can make a profound difference.

Charms: Start a charm bracelet for your friend with charms that have meaning and inspiration, with words like *courage, just believe,* and so on. Each week you can add a new inspiring thought or image.

Promises: Make a checklist of things you promise to do for your friend. "This week I promise to come over and wash all the sheets in your house."

Foodstuffs: Make a tuna sandwich and fill a Thermos with hot tea and deliver it to your friend during one of her chemotherapy treatments.

Listening: Don't feel you have to offer advice. What your friend probably wants most is someone just to listen to her.

The End in Sight

*One Brave Woman Discovers That Meaning Lies in the
Here and Now*

It is only with the heart that one sees rightly.
—Antoine de Saint-Exupéry

Imagine being told at age twenty-four that you will spend most
of your adulthood blind. "Do whatever you can now, because
you won't be able to see by the time you are forty," Kathy Austin
remembers the doctor telling her.

"I didn't believe him," she recalls. "Looking back, I guess I
realized that by the end of high school I knew something was
beginning to be wrong with my eyes, but I was in shock and just
refused to believe that could happen to me."

Eleven months later, the Homewood/Flossmoor, Illinois woman
walked down the aisle to marry Bryan. Soon afterward their
daughter Missy was born, followed by son Bryan.

Kathy was diagnosed with the retinitis pigmentosa, a heredi-
tary degenerative disease of the retina. No one else in her family
suffers from the condition.

Gradually and relentlessly it began robbing her sight, like a
shadow moving across the TV screen. By age twenty-eight, she
began losing her reading vision. When little Bryan was in first
grade, she could no longer curl up with her children on her lap
to read them stories.

Today, at age forty-nine, this mom of two—Missy, twenty-
three, and Bryan, seventeen, is nearly 100 percent blind. She
only sees slight shadows. Together with her yellow Lab Jethro,
Kathy commutes from her south suburban Chicago home to her
Michigan Avenue job in the city as Adult Rehabilitation Services

Coordinator for the Guild for the Blind. She also volunteers several days a month to work with the city of Chicago's training program for taxicab drivers. The program instructs cab drivers on how to be sensitive to the blind and is in place in large part because of drivers' hesitation to pick up blind people and allow the dogs into their cabs, Kathy explains.

"There are not a lot of resources for adults who become blind. I struggled a lot to find help. That's why now I am all about trying to educate people about ways to help the blind live vital and full lives."

In December 2005 she graduated from Roosevelt University in Chicago with a 4.0 GPA and received the President's Award for Excellence in Scholarship and Leadership from Prairie State College, where she had received her associates degree, also with a 4.0 in 2003. This award was for overall involvement with the college; she was active in student government and held a leadership role in an organization called "Label Us Able."

Most who meet Kathy are immediately struck by her profound braveness, steely determination to live life to its fullest, and the fact that she doesn't "look blind."

She explains, "Because I lost my sight later in life, I know how to look people in their face when they are talking and I have some light perception and see some contrasts. People don't always realize I am blind."

Only infrequently does she allow herself to indulge in the fact that she is painfully aware of the losses and limitations.

"Sometimes I get sad because I don't know what my children look like; the last memories I have of them is when Bryan was five. I can't look at his senior portrait. And when parents complain about having to carpool, I just think I would kill to drive a carpool. But I'm blessed with an extremely supportive family, and we've strived from the beginning not to make my blindness an issue."

Kathy hopes to bring attention to the needs of the blind and to gently teach people what to do and say. She remembers one time when she was commuting on the train to her job and the train conductor took her ticket, then took her hand and spelled t-h-a-n-k y-o-u into the palm of her hand. Kathy laughs, "Some people mean well, and you have to laugh, but many assume I am blind and deaf. I try not to get offended."

She says her biggest challenge has been "not having someone to talk to" outside of family and close friends. "I think because my sight loss was so gradual, I made the mistake early on of always acting like I was okay, like I could do it all myself. I didn't force myself to call on my friends and family to help me learn more about what I would be facing in the years ahead." Kathy says she is lucky. She has a group of girlfriends who recently made sure she was included in the girls' weekend away in Michigan and invited her to be part of the golf foursome and ride along in the cart to enjoy a great day outside.

Words to Live By

"There are not a lot of resources for adults who become blind. I struggled a lot to try to find help. That's why now I am all about trying to educate people about ways to help the blind live vital and full lives."

Kathy's Tips for Helping a Friend Who Is Visually Impaired

Avoid being a "body snatcher." Blind people are always being grabbed and pulled around. It's very uncomfortable and hard to know what to say to ask someone not to do that. So it's best to avoid the pushing and pulling.

Ask first. Ask a blind person if they need help before you assume they do and start doing it for him or her.

Walk on. If the blind person does ask you to help guide him or her, the best way to do that is to offer your left elbow and stay about a half step behind.

Speak up. When you're ending a conversation and walking on to another group of people at a cocktail party, don't leave without saying so. It's embarrassing to think the sighted person is still standing there and then find you are talking to no one.

Calm your fears. Don't be afraid to say things like "See you later" or "Nice seeing you today."

Treat us the same. Just because we've lost our sight doesn't mean we're different. We try to live just like everyone else.

Dispel the myths. People always ask if my hearing has gotten better. No, but yes, I probably have learned to pay closer attention to what I hear.

Armed with Humor

A Thirty-Something Woman Faces Fear and Passion Head On by Drawing Friends Near to Laugh

From moment to moment, one can bear much.
— Teresa of Avila

The subject line on the CarePage: "Vote on your favorite Dolly wig."

The message: "Hi all. I am still in the hospital, and will probably be here for a while. No one has started talking about me going home anytime soon. My blood levels, after the chemo, are very low, and because my white blood cell count is .010, they want to keep me on constant IV antibiotics. I was thinking of a Dolly Parton blonde wig. What do you think?"

These are the first entries on Cara's CarePage in January 2006, when she entered the hospital after being diagnosed with leukemia. For ten years before, she had struggled with kidney failure and had already had two kidney transplants. For the next months, she would write daily, many times a day, from her room, 1017 Elevator C on the oncology ward at Rush University Medical Center in Chicago.

Because she was in isolation for so much of the time, her umbilical cord to the outside world was a relic computer in the visitor's lounge. That's when she was having "a good day," and doctors allowed her to escape the confines of her sealed room. Or, when a downloaded virus hadn't tripped up the computer. Or, when she could squeeze in between swarms of visiting families and tap into the only joyful messages she was getting these days.

On the days that she found her way to the computer and clicked on her CarePages Web postings that are on her Web site—CaringforCara—she found notes from an army of friends, colleagues, family members, and even strangers. She knew she was not alone. These messages played the leading role in her imagery of recovery, Cara told me.

"It's the only place where I get strength and know that my friends and family are holding me and loving me all the time," she said.

At the time, we talked about how much she wanted to be back in her place in Lincoln Park, in the grandstands at Wrigley Field, sitting in snarled traffic on the Eden's Expressway en route to work at Hewitt Associates in Lincolnshire—anywhere but the room where the door must always be closed and the limited visitors must don plastic gloves and be vigilant about their own health. Sniffles are a big deal on the tenth floor of oncology.

But never mind the cathport that courses chemotherapy through her veins or the kidneys her body has rejected in the last ten years. Never mind the blow that came on Christmas Eve 2005, when, weeks after celebrating the two-year anniversary of her second successful transplant, a funny pain in her side prompted doctors to insist she jump in a cab and head across town to the Chicago medical center. In the early hours of the morning, alone in the ER, a nurse delivered the bad news: a tumor on her native kidney, and leukemia.

Chemo didn't kill the deadly invaders. To the contrary, they kept multiplying. Family members, most of whom lived out of state, flew in to test as donors for the life-saving bone marrow transplant. It was touted as "the miracle" by the nonstop procession of white lab coats that poked needles in and out of Cara around the clock. A week after her physician brother from Phoenix arrived and was identified as a donor, the surgery was cancelled. Her immune system was too compromised.

But the irrepressible Cara was always singing in her soul. She had no tolerance for self-pity. If anything, all this made her faster, and funnier.

Humor—her own, and the funny, uplifting messages from friends—has been her armor, she confided at the time.

Like many single thirty-somethings in pursuit of the ultimate soul mate, she and her friends joked going into the hospital: "Hey, maybe you'll meet a cute doctor, your own Dr. McDreamy."

None of the surgical residents seemed to fit the bill. And Cara, clutching a towel she kept plastered on her head in an effort to stave off the clumps of her auburn hair that kept falling out, protested, "I'm not exactly the most attractive these days." That's when friends *did* ignore her. They posted photos of cute docs on her Web site.

The Web postings were her lifeline and made a big difference, said Cara. Trying to feel as normal as possible is the best way she finds to cope. Observers who haven't been clued in would never know that the messages are powerful antidotes to the exhaustion of chemotherapy.

She wrote, "This past weekend was really nice. I had a few visitors throughout the days, and then was able to nap in between. I am a little embarrassed to admit this, but on Sunday, I had my eyebrows done, semi-professionally, for the first time. Sarves and Farah came to visit and Farah pulled out the 'thread,' and threaded them for me. . . . They look so nice! Thanks again Farah. (It's the little things at this point!)"

For the friends who got to sit at Cara's bedside "on the good days," Cara was steel, the strength. The friends forged a secret pact—to keep their tears out of her e-mails and the cloak of comfort they struggle to wrap around her. They would bump into each other in coffee shops, hug and cry over lattes. They visited boutique wig shops and clipped articles about chemo-caps out of their Sunday papers. They pounded their fists and dialed cell phones: "What can we do for Cara?"

They sat at her bedside and watched a friend with an illness that compromised everything, and they stumbled and stuttered when she would tiptoe into an area she had forbidden herself to go: "How will someone love me, when I have all this wrong with me?" The friend wouldn't know what to say, except to tell Cara that many people love her, that Mr. Right probably won't be found rocking out at Cubby Bear, a popular bar across from Wrigley Field. But he will be that special guy who will love a woman who has faced the unimaginable and met her challenge with dignity, determination, strength, and guts.

The friends would leave the hospital and let the tears pour out. For Cara's circle of friends, the year was filled with the lessons of death and learning instead to celebrate life and memories that live on forever.

Cara was mentor to this group of pals who were known for throwing great parties. They gathered in September 2005 to say good-bye to buddy Ann, our friend, a mom of three, and a wife who lost her battle with ovarian cancer. It was Cara who organized the farewell car caravan to St. Louis to the funeral. Cara was the first to call when my next-door neighbor, Vince, the guy who served the beer and reveled in his latest marinade creations, died unexpectedly at age fifty.

The living need to keep on going, Cara insisted.

So many people want to do a good deed, to help. The purple and azure handmade shawl, stitched by a group of women from Cara's mother's Catholic parish, provided much more than warmth for Cara and underscored dozens of gestures that made a big difference in how she felt.

In the corner of her room was a freestanding "spiritual bouquet" that was delivered and made by her sister Cathleen. It carried dozens of special prayers and messages she collected from all of her friends and family.

Getting By with a Little Help from Friends

Ties to a close network of friends create a social safety net that is good for society and for the individual. Research has linked social support and community to healing.

But some days, fear couldn't help but slam her boundless energy and perky spirit.

On Valentine's Day 2006, Cara wrote, "Doctors and nurses are trying to figure out what is best to do at this point. I know there are no definite answers in any book, so I'm doing my best to be a good patient and understand their thinking about some of their treatment options, i.e., one of the meds they are about to give me is known to be toxic to the kidneys. So far, I've been really lucky to not have any complications with my kidney, but to think about the real possibility of losing this one and having to go through all of that again truly upsets me and makes me feel pretty scared."

Sadly Cara lost her battle with leukemia on December 1, 2006. She was thirty-seven when she died.

Words to Live By

"It's the only place where I get strength and know that my friends and family are holding me and loving me all the time."

Serving Up Solace and Support
Now It's Their Turn

It is well to give when asked, but it is better
to give unasked, through understanding.
—Kahlil Gibran

Tom and Amy Hills have always been the strong ones, the couple others could count on when a family member became ill, or there was a death among their church congregation. Amy and Tom staffed the phone chains, served up dinners for the families, and picked up the kids whenever and wherever they were needed.

But, when cancer struck close to home, Amy and Tom had to learn to do the illness role reversal, step back, and let others come calling to care for them. Here they share their experience.

Late on a Friday afternoon in October 2004, Amy and Tom Hills stood together and reluctantly pledged into a fast-growing fraternity: the Order of Couples Battling Breast Cancer.

"What bothered me the most was that all of a sudden some people started treating us differently, as if we were 'the cancer couple,'" recalls Tom. "People you hardly know would come up to you and you could just see the look of pity in their eyes. They'd get this death-knell tone and ask, 'So how old are your children?' and you knew where they were going with that—that the kids would graduate from high school without their mom."

But the Ft. Thomas, Kentucky, couple had no intention of hanging out at the cancer frat party for long.

Tough-minded and determined, the word *survivor* became part of their vocabulary from the get-go. Forming a united front, they boldly stared in the face of the statistics that say 40,000 American men and women die of breast cancer each year. They took their stance: "Nope, not us."

"We wanted to show from the beginning what is possible," says Tom.

Amy and Tom's overriding goal: to make life as normal as possible for their three children: Ryan, sixteen; Stephanie, fifteen; and Abby, twelve, at the time of diagnosis.

A brigade of friends, neighbors, and church members stepped up to embrace, support, and help the family climb up the looming mountain of cancer. This army of culinary crusaders, with a neighbor leading the charge, collected their recipes and delivered home-cooked meals to the Hills' household every other week for months throughout Amy's chemotherapy treatments.

Another friend orchestrated a team to drive Amy back and forth to the treatments so that she would never be alone. Cards—a couple hundred of them—poured in daily, as did the messages on the couple's Web page offering concern and compassion.

"People were phenomenal," says Amy. "If I was having a hard day, I'd look at their messages or listen to the messages on the phone, and I would be so inspired and feel so much better."

She says she also had great doctors and nurses who were "very caring."

"Listening to the patient and answering their questions without trying to get them out the door quickly is really important," says Amy.

"The extra touch of caring was the phone call I received after my first chemo treatment from my oncology nurse, wanting to know how I was feeling," she says.

Right before her chemotherapy, Amy's friends threw a "chemo shower." That same night, the guys took Tom out. Friends walked in the door with everything from inspirational books, handmade scarves, and a chenille comforter to gift certificates for massages, pizza delivery coupons, and a dinner out for her and Tom. One woman gave her a basket brimming with all the little things that she would need from the store—the daily stuff moms are always driving to get, including cards for her to send to others, so that she wouldn't skip a beat. Another neighbor washed and folded the family laundry while Amy was at chemo.

Looking back, both Amy and Tom agree it was hard at first to accept help from well-meaning friends. Both were used to being the doers, the casserole deliverers.

"I wanted to keep everything as normal as possible for our kids," says Amy. "It was tough at first to accept the offers of 'What can I do to help you?' because I'm usually the one bringing the casseroles," says Amy. "But, I figured this is one time in my life that it was okay to accept help from people. And I discovered they were so thrilled to be able to help. They wanted something tangible they could do to help."

Tom also remembers being determined: "I'm going to do it all." He even studied for the task, leafing through *Breast Cancer Husband* as his "invaluable" road map for the next two years. Tom is a marketing executive whose job requires frequent travel across the country, but his boss and colleagues insisted he stay put at home and be with Amy and the kids. They doubled their schedules and took over all of his travel and sales calls. Thank God, everyone ignored his insistence to do it all, Tom now says.

These days, Amy and Tom have tapped into the joyful energy that was sent their way and are letting it float back to others. Amy has found that her openness and positive attitude have encouraged other women to schedule breast exams. It's helped Amy and Tom's friends know that cancer can be dealt with proactively.

Words to Live By

"I wanted to keep everything as normal as possible for our kids," says Amy. "It was tough at first to accept the offers of 'What can I do to help you?' because I'm usually the one bringing the casseroles."

▶ Getting Started: The Inside Track on Carrying Each Other

For those of us who have suffered or watched the pain and sorrow of illness, it is sometimes very hard to understand the deeper meaning, to glimpse where we fit in to help. "Why?" we ask. "This doesn't seem fair." And yet, we got e-mails from Cara, who from her room in isolation on the oncology ward asked us to help her help others by setting up *CarePages.com* sites for them. At the same time that she was a support giver, she became the one who needs messages of support. The way she knows others are there for her was to log on to the Internet.

We are inclined to want to fix it for anyone suffering, but we have come to learn that there is a life force inside them that frees them to be fully who they truly are, even in the worst of times, and to be at peace. It will forever remain a mystery. All we can do is listen; listen to their stories, and be present in whatever way the mystery unfolds. It is a gift to be asked to share someone's pain. It is our challenge to find the opening to genuine compassion.

From the CarePages Frontlines

Creating the Magic of Caring: These Chemo-Fairies Give New Meaning to Helping

"I read about this and have done it twice. When two of my friends were going through chemotherapy, we organized a group of chemo-fairies who would leave gifts at the front door after each session. When the chemotherapy sessions were over and our friends were feeling better, we had a surprise dinner to share who the chemo-fairies were and celebrate. Now a coworker has been diagnosed, and we have both men and women who want to participate. The guys weren't crazy about the name and someone recommended chemo-sabis."
—*Linda Pelliccioni*

Tangible Things You Can Do to Lighten a Mom's Load

"If the woman has children, do things to help keep the kids' lives as normal as possible. Offer to make their school lunches

throughout her chemo treatments (big job—perhaps team up with another mom). If you are taking your child shopping for a Halloween costume, offer to take her children, too. Pick up a gift for her child to take to the birthday party. I am not suggesting you pay for all of these things, but do the legwork on her behalf."
— *Lynn Fletcher*

Creating a Basket of Wishes
"I was diagnosed right before the end of the school year. My teaching colleagues knew that they couldn't be with me through my surgery (and what came after it) because we would be on summer vacation. Unbeknownst to me, they collected cards and small gifts and put them in a large basket. The basket was presented to me at our end-of-the-year meeting. I had one card/gift to open for each day of summer vacation. It helped me tremendously to know that I had the thoughts and prayers of so many other women!"
— *Rebecca Gardner*

CHAPTER 5

ACTS OF KINDNESS

Sometimes It's the Little Things That Count

The life I touch for good or ill will touch
another life and that in turn another, until
who knows where the trembling stops or
in what far place my touch will be felt.
— Frederick Buechner

You can't know how others will respond to you in crisis until the world drops out from under you. In this chapter, we shine the spotlight on people who know how to behave in the wake of tragedy. They simply show up and deliver their acts of kindness. And then they leave, not expecting you to do anything for them.

The Circle of Life Support
Gifts Carry the Story of Hope and Healing

If the world is to be healed through human efforts, I am convinced it will be by ordinary people, people whose love for this life is even greater than their fear. People who can open to the web of life that called us into being, and who can rest in the vitality of that larger body.
—Joanne Macy

When crisis happens, many of us become numb. In this story, one mom learns to gather fresh reserves of courage and hope from the cadre of people who swarmed like worker bees to her family's rescue.

Catherine Wilcox endured many sleepless nights after her son Isaac, now five, was injured in a car accident in November 2004. For three months, the Howell, Michigan, mother of three and her husband lived in Isaac's hospital room as he fought for his life. Today, Isaac is dependent on a ventilator to breathe and is quadriplegic. Catherine says the family survives one day at a time, determined to do whatever they can to give Isaac a normal life.

For Catherine and her family, what got them through "this chaotic time in our lives" were the simple acts of kindness that became and still are a multitude of blessings day after day.

For instance, Catherine remembers her bosses, so distressed at hearing about the accident and not knowing what to do, filled a huge hospital survival care package brimming with everything the family might need during their lengthy hospital stay: magazines, puzzle books, toiletries, snacks, toys for Isaac's brothers, and flexible Spiderman figures that included suction cups so that they could be attached to Isaac's bed to cheer him up when he emerged from his coma.

Focused on being present for Isaac around the clock, visitors "were not on our most-wanted list," recalls Catherine.

Instead, the messages of support that poured in on their CarePage, "IsaacDaniel," and through cards and letters became the family's lifeline.

"When someone takes the time to write something out, it is usually heartfelt," says Catherine. "It was also convenient for us to open greetings and well-wishes when time and circumstance provided the opportunity, amid tests and monitors and medications and questions and explanations and bad news and an endless stream of medical professionals."

The messages were especially powerful, she said, on days when they heard discouraging news. "We would find hope, blessings, and prayers," she remembers. A stream of balloons, flowers, and cuddly stuffed animals helped bring life and vitality to the hospital room.

Sometimes, like Catherine, you just want someone to help you forget the pain, to make you laugh, to tell you stories, and most important, to offer you new hope.

That person or persons and their presence become a gift.

We all have a longing to give. And sometimes, when someone does something for us—a note, a phone call—we are comforted and reminded of what we have to offer someone else. Here we share our favorite tips on how to carry each other.

Tips to Give and Share: Thirty Comforting Ideas from Our CarePages House to Yours

We asked our CarePages' family and friends to share with us some of the simple yet unique ways they have found to give of their hearts to others. We know that little things do make a difference and hope these thoughtful ideas will inspire our readers.

1. *Comfort food and a time-out.* "After our seventeen-year-old daughter, Liz, went through a twelve-hour spinal fusion surgery, all of our friends and family rallied around us. But it was interesting to note how differently folks perceived the intensity of what we were experiencing. Everyone was wonderful with support, but it was clear there were some who didn't quite understand how all-encompassing this mega-surgery was to Liz, and ultimately, to us. One of those who totally 'got it' was Irma, the mother of one of Liz's best friends, Christy. About the sixth day Liz was in the hospital, Christy came to visit her, along with her mom, an amazing, nurturing woman whose claim to fame among Liz and her friends is the incredible spreads of food she'll supply to the kids when they're at their house. Irma is a fabulous cook who rarely, if ever, eats on the run and was horrified to learn that Ray and I had eaten nothing but hospital cafeteria food for nearly a week. She insisted that she would watch over Liz and *ordered* us to go get a real dinner. The *ordering* part is important; if she simply had offered, we probably would have declined. Now, leaving Liz's bedside was something we hadn't done since she was hospitalized, simply because we never felt comfortable leaving her alone. We checked with Liz, not knowing if she'd get upset if we left, and when she assured us that she'd be fine, we walked across the street from the medical center (Rush Medical Center in Chicago) to a restaurant inside the Marriott Hotel. For the first time in days, we ate food that wasn't chosen from the hospital cafeteria buffet line. We were only gone about an hour, and I don't even remember what I ate, but that dinner felt like a gourmet, five-star meal. We had a glass of wine and returned to the hospital feeling more human and relaxed and ever-so-

grateful to this lovely woman who stayed by our daughter's bedside so we could have a bit of a reprieve. The moral of the story is that when you're dealing with long hospital stays, it can be an immense treat to have someone stay with your child to give you an hour outside the confines of the hospital." (Ann Franczak, Inverness, Illinois)

2. *Don't be afraid to get it wrong.* A friend who lost her husband during the past year tells us about all the people who disappeared weeks after the funeral. The phone stopped ringing, and only vague references on getting together are mentioned if friends accidentally bump into her at the grocery store. She tells us, "I wish they weren't afraid of getting it wrong, because that would be better than disappearing." Friends who have lost a loved one often are very lonely. Send a gift certificate for dinner and then offer to be the date.

3. *Provide a dose of delight.* Take your friend on an excursion to a "delightful place"—a botanical garden, nature trail, beach, forest preserve. There is something very soul soothing about the smells of flowers, eucalyptus trees, fresh-cut grass, a lake or ocean.

4. *Make it a quick visit.* For a friend who is seriously ill and housebound, drop off some food, books, or videos, but make sure you don't overstay your welcome.

5. *Help with everyday tasks.* When our friend Pam got in an auto accident that put her temporarily in a wheelchair, a group of friends rallied to the rescue to help schedule dinner deliveries to her house, arrange rides for her eighth-grade

son to and from school and football practice, and even to escort her to the manicurist.

6. *Make your own kind of music.* "I was at Ravinia (an outdoor concert venue on Chicago's North Shore) recently, watching a lot of daughters walking their elderly parents around the grounds. It's nice to see people trying to get their parents out to enjoy the simple pleasures of life, like a summer evening of music. I hope my kids are as attentive to me when I get old. What are some special places your elderly parents or a friend might like to go for an evening or day away from their worries and medical ails? Museum? Library? Coffee shop?" (Laurie D. Borman, Highwood, Illinois)

7. *Spread the word.* "It is hard for the family to contact every single person. Once someone contacts you, offer to call other friends and neighbors. It can be exhausting for the family trying to let everyone know that a loved one has passed away." (Valerie Johnson, senior, University of Iowa)

8. *Cool it.* Recently, when a friend lost her father and dozens of out-of-town relatives descended upon her house for the three-day duration of the wake, funeral, and aftermath, a bunch of friends set up coolers in their backyard stocked with pop and water which proved to be a godsend. Every morning, the cooler fillers arrived with a fresh bag of drinks and ice to replenish.

9. *Drive the love boat.* If relatives are arriving from out of town for a funeral or to say their last good-byes, offer to be the chauffeur and transport them from the airport, train station, or to pick up elderly relatives from their homes.

10. *Provide food for the soul.* Whether you're feeding a family while one of its members is in the hospital or nourishing out-of-towners for a funeral, there is no better gift than home-made food. Organize a pool of chefs to cook up comfort food to give and share, and make sure you've got a team in place to create your own meals-on-wheels network.

11. *Pay it forward.* "I know a family that could not afford to buy the plane tickets to travel to their mother/grandmother's funeral. A generous friend gave them a check to cover the transportation costs. It is something to think about instead of flowers or a charity." (Valerie Johnson, senior, University of Iowa)

12. *Create "I care" packages.* Giving joy is found in the simple things—special little treasures that will renew—a paperback book, scented candle, movie coupon, bubble bath, flowers, magazines, crossword puzzles, books.

13. *Knit with love.* For centuries, women have relied on knitting to calm themselves and form circles of community. Following the death of a friend's husband, a group decided to gather in his honor with knitting needles, yarn, and a desire to do good in hand. They formed an informal group that meets regularly and donates scarves to battered women across the country. The scarves make the women who receive them feel pretty, and it helps the grieving group of friends, stitch by stitch, make a difference.

14. *Provide entertainment.* Offer to take a sick friend to the movies. Or bring over a DVD, make some popcorn, and watch a funny movie together.

15. *Become the wheels.* Offer to accompany your friend to his or her medical appointment.

16. *Speak up with compassion.* Leave a voice message or e-mail letting her know she isn't forgotten, that you love her.

17. *Serve an ounce of comfort.* "I had no idea it would be our last 'spot of tea' together. My grandmother, bedridden for the past six months, told me she just wanted a cup of tea for lunch. A staple of our Irish family's culinary expertise, tea was something they consumed every day. My mother was my grandmother's sole around-the-clock caregiver. We had watched Grandma shrink from 125 pounds down to less than 100. And the afternoon she asked for tea was the day that I, the granddaughter, was leaving for Arizona State University and my freshman year in college. We sipped tea. She reached out her hand, and told me, "Mayie, there is a whole world out there waiting for you." I kissed my grandmother good-bye and hopped on a plane. And three hours later, when I called from the pay phone at the Phoenix airport, she had moved to heaven." (Mary Beth Sammons)

18. *Create brilliant arrangements.* Send flowers, lots of them. Nancy Lawlor, a New York clerical temp, came up with a "brilliant arrangement." She convinced Manhattan hoteliers to turn over pink roses, lilies, and bouquets of flowers to be delivered to local hospitals to cheer up patients who were particularly isolated. Today, her efforts have blossomed into FlowerPower, a nonprofit that delivers these arrangements to patients in hospices, nursing homes, and hospitals. Check it out at *www.flowerpowerfoundation.org.*

19. *Throw a feel-good shower.* Mary Ellen and her friends came up with a great idea that was practical and helpful for one of their girlfriends who was about to undergo intensive radiation and chemotherapy for breast cancer. They threw a hat shower. Everyone was invited to bring along a cute hat and an inspirational letter for their friend.

20. *Put together a get-well kit.* Include in your kit bottled water, green tea, Kleenex, and a bundle of healthy remedies: chicken noodle soup, fruits, vitamin C, echinacea. Go to the health food store. Get inspired.

21. *Stretch yourself.* If you're the caregiver, take time to renew and refresh. Breathe deep, cultivate physical health and wellness and spiritual sustenance with yoga.

22. *Offer healing touch.* Massage can be a powerful tool for creating change and calming our psyches on a very deep level. Purchase a gift certificate for a massage for your friend that can be redeemed when he or she is able.

23. *Launch a caring project in your friend's honor.* Several years ago, shortly after a friend died in her young forties from breast cancer, a group of us formed a team and walked in the Avon Three-Day Breast Cancer Walk. Across the country, friends and relatives are opting to bond while bettering the world on behalf of a friend or loved ones to help fight disease.

24. *Send a box of inspiration.* Empower your friend or loved one by providing them with a box filled with inspirational books, inspiring quotes, or music.

25. *Think outside of the box.* Recently when Beth's cousin was losing his battle with lung cancer and the medical bills were mounting, friends threw a surprise afternoon party at a local eatery. Discovering it was also his and his wife's twenty-fifth anniversary, they brought in a preacher to help them celebrate their anniversary by renewing their vows. There wasn't a dry eye in the place.

26. *Give her a smile.* "One day when I was returning to work after my chemo treatment (I was on my prep period from my teaching job), I was a little down. I was also going through a divorce after more than twenty-three years of marriage. While on the highway, a nice-looking young man looked over at me as he passed my car and gave me a big smile. That smile really made my day. He will never know what a lift it gave me at that low moment I was having. A smile can be a powerful thing. I try to share one whenever I can. Thanks, young man, wherever you are." (Joyce Bates)

27. *Show up.* "When my best friend was going through treatment for breast cancer, we did a number of things to try to be helpful. We bought a small freezer for her family then held cook-in-bulk get-togethers to fill it with easily heated prepared meals. We hired someone to come and clean her house a couple of times a month. We tried to make a point of talking to her as a whole person. She really resented feeling that she was being defined by cancer. And she wanted to continue being a friend, keeping up her part of the give and take of friendship. If we tried to shield her too much or help too much, she felt isolated. We laughed as much as possible. Someone she worked with gave her an anonymous gift of cash with instructions to spend it

on herself and, later, to pass it on, if she had the chance."
(CarePage member)

28. *Create moments of "life as normal."* "My dearest friend had
    breast cancer, and over time, the issue that bothered her the
    most was the lack of normalcy in her life. She was an avid
    baker prior to her diagnosis and treatment, and she really
    missed baking. So, with Christmas coming, and her still
    recovering from a bone marrow transplant months before,
    I asked her if she would like to have a "Baking Day." She
    was thrilled. She got her recipes out, I shopped for the
    ingredients, and when the day came, happily it was a good
    day and she was feeling well. I created an "assembly line"
    on her countertop with each of the ingredients in order, so
    that she could simply roll from one ingredient to the next
    (she was still wheelchair bound). When it came to stirring,
    often I had to help, but that was okay, because at the end
    of the day, we had cakes, pies, cookies, and candies that she
    had made! Her husband and daughter were thrilled to have
    Mom's delicacies, and she was so proud! The next day we
    froze some items, and later on, we had a "Gift Basket Day,"
    during which we took the items from the freezer, set up
    another assembly line, and she made food baskets as pres-
    ents for her friends and family. It gave her a sense of inde-
    pendence, since she didn't feel like shopping but she was
    able to give presents that she had made herself. It was such
    a wonderful experience for me, and I believe, from all of the
    smiles she gave me, for her as well." (Tammy Shropshire)

29. *Create a groundswell of support.* "My mother and sister came
    to my appointments even if I said I didn't need them. This
    helped support me in times that were difficult. One of them

would come over on my worst days to just be here just in case I needed anything. There is no repaying that kind of support! A friend asked if I needed anything or needed meals, I responded no. The next day she e-mailed me a list of dates and people who were delivering meals. She picked up my son from school, along with her carpool, and I didn't have to think about coordinating anything! This was such a relief. Another good friend threw a surprise birthday party for my daughter when I couldn't celebrate her special day myself! This same friend came over the day I was diagnosed, bringing flowers and an incredible note, and just dropped them off and left, which was perfect. Another friend that I didn't even know very well brought over dinners continuously with her daughter. Another mother and daughter made a special dinner that was set up like a picnic that brought smiles to my whole family! When I was in the hospital for six days, I didn't really care to eat, but people brought snacks, and that helped me. Another called and asked what kind of sleepwear I liked and brought some great soft nightgowns. A few friends came over and planted flowers in the spring when I couldn't do it. My house was a mess, and some helped by sending cleaners or doing it themselves. It was hard to accept all this help, but it was needed and was *sooooo* appreciated! There were so many gifts and great things that I can't even list them all. My husband tried to take care of so many things. It helped when people called or e-mailed with special messages. One acquaintance sent a bag of goodies and also sent a list of quotes that always helped her." (Selessa Holmberg)

30. *Pray.* Sometimes all you can do is be still and offer a prayer to God or the universe to step in and do the caring for you.

CHAPTER 6

GIVE WHAT YOU HAVE

It's All We Can Do

Compassion is the basis of morality.
—Arthur Schopenhauer, German philosopher

We sometimes need to think about caring for someone who is ill or has experienced loss in a new way.

Caring for someone else doesn't always mean changing your career to become a full-time nurse or that you need suddenly to become a gourmet chef serving up dinners every night of the week for a sick person's family.

One of the greatest gifts we can give in a time of crisis is the part of us that makes us unique. For some, our most expert talents and skills—writing letters, drafting legal documents, taking care of small children, or giving massages—may be exactly what someone else needs. A widow might need a lawyer to help with the estate. Maybe our gift with gardening—planting or arranging flowers—can help ease someone else's pain.

Healing Touch
A Friend Offers Medicine for the Soul

Friendship is a sheltering tree.
—Samuel Taylor Coleridge

At some moments, we just know instinctively what needs to be done to care for a friend in need. It is these spontaneous gestures that often become healing moments that speak louder than any words.

A friend, Ann, was dying of ovarian cancer. Less than a year before, this thirty-seven-year-old St. Louis, Missouri, woman had given birth to her third child, a son. Now, she lay in a hospital bed and later at home. Krista Burke, her best friend, had traveled from Arlington Heights, Illinois, to Ann's bedside.

Krista would sit for very long times at Ann's bedside, leaning close to her and listening and talking about the realness and rawness of what was happening. It seemed to give Ann some real grounding, a sense of normalcy, while day after day she battled the disease and the roller coaster of emotions that went with it.

One day close to the end, when Ann was back in the hospital and her husband, kids, and relatives happened to be away, Krista found herself alone with Ann. Krista talked. Ann talked a little and rested a lot. Dying is horrible. Krista held Ann's hand and then did the only thing she thought she could do to provide comfort—she gave her a foot massage. This simple gesture enabled Krista to embody her support and love for her friend.

Words to Live By

"Dying is horrible. Krista held Ann's hand and then did the only thing she thought she could do to provide comfort—she gave her a foot massage."

You're Beautiful, It's True!
Beauty Expert Helps Teens Battle Cancer

We can't help everyone, but everyone can help someone.
—Dr. Coretta Scott King

If you've ever had a doubt about the power of the simple things to make a big difference in the lives of those coping with illness, you haven't met Lori Ovitz. A sought-after makeup artist to the stars, Lori knows a lot about beauty. And as wife to Bruce, a thirty-five-year cancer survivor, she knows firsthand how the right actions done at just the right moment can offer inspiration and bring a smile to the faces of those coping with cancer.

Lori is committed to the belief that cancer does not have to rob you of self-esteem or beauty. That belief gave her the impetus to travel to cancer wards and cancer support group organizations throughout the Chicago area, and these days the country, helping to teach cancer patients how to apply makeup so that they can learn to face the mirror confidently and embrace life again by using makeup to make a difference. She's also written the book Facing the Mirror with Cancer.

"I've seen firsthand what an incredible transformation occurs in their appearance and how much better they feel about themselves," says the Chicago resident.

Here we walk with Lori as she wields her magic with a group of teens with cancer (15,000 American teens are currently undergoing treatment). Lori's experience underscores that all of us have unique talents and abilities and if we use a little imagination, we can find that they too can make a big—or little, but significant—difference in the life of a loved one, or even a stranger facing illness or loss.

When thirteen-year-old Rachel Miller learned she had cancer, the blow struck hard. Beyond the emotional roller coaster of life-threatening illness and a year spent in hospitals instead of school, gymnastics, and movies with friends, the knockdown was losing her hair.

"The face I saw wasn't me," recalls Rachel. "I just froze. It scared me so much. I hid because I didn't want my friends to come over and see me."

"It's hard enough to be a teen these days, but for teens with cancer, all they want to do is to be able to go out and look like themselves," says Lori Ovitz.

On this day, Lori worked her magic with beauty tricks— chocolate lipsticks, eyebrow pencils, and fake eyelashes—for Rachel and about a dozen other teenage girls and their moms who gathered at the University of Chicago Comer Children's Hospital for a spa pampering workshop.

"I feel so pretty," says a beaming Gigi Lopez, a fifteen-year-old freshman from East Chicago, as she held up the mirror and smiled. "Wow, this is the first time I looked in the mirror and didn't cry."

An eye-shadowed, lip-glossed Rachel says at the time how she now was looking forward to her upcoming graduation trip aboard the *Odyssey*, a ship that provides nightly dinner cruises on Lake Michigan.

"I'm excited," says Rachel. "Only, my mom says I'm still going to have to wear flat shoes, which I don't like."

Lori volunteers weekly at Comer (and frequently gives workshops at hospitals across the country). Her goal: to help teens feel pretty on the outside so they can readjust their internal self-confidence mirror.

"I'm trying to help give them a sense of control and renewed confidence so that they can get back to the social life teens love best," says Lori.

"This is very healing, because all they want to be is to just be normal teens again," said Sarah Karela. "It helps their inside beauty shine on the outside."

Words to Live By

"It's hard enough to be a teen these days, but for teens with cancer, all they want to do is to be able to go out and look like themselves."

A Gift for Words

Remember, if you ever need a helping hand, you'll find one at the end of your arm. As you grow older you will discover that you have two hands. One for helping yourself, the other for helping others.
— Audrey Hepburn

If you're having trouble finding a way to help a friend or family member through a time of sorrow, consider the example of Sally, a Michigan mom of three grown children, who has learned over and over again how much the right words can mean for others during times when life has handed them moments of inconsolable grief. She's got a gift for words and knows that a card, a note, or a simple message can become a lifeline—a permanent, tangible reference that you care. And, the great thing is you may be able to write things you aren't comfortable saying face to face. If you've ever received this kind of letter, you know the goose bumps it brings. Think of how that felt and let it inspire you to pen words of caring and comfort for someone who needs them.

Tragedies experienced by three close friends who had all lost their young sons—two to illness and one in an automobile accident—jolted Sally into action to find the right words and responses to help ease the hurt. That is when she discovered the power of the right words spoken at the right moment to transform.

"In my mind, that's a parent's worst nightmare," Sally remembers thinking. "I tried to make it a point to 'be there' for them, by extending hugs, which I felt was the most comforting thing one can do. And, I tried to continue to let them know that I would help them to honor their sons' memories and to celebrate their lives by sharing stories and experiences."

Years later, Sally still tries to send the right words and thoughts of comfort—in a card, or sometimes again, just with a hug, on the anniversary of her friends' sons' deaths.

She says, "My daughter teases me that I send cards to the milkman. She knows I tend to buy cards (of all varieties) to have on hand for different purposes. I know of a couple of people who are undergoing cancer treatments and who are seriously ill."

These days, in addition to doing whatever else she can, Sally tries to send cards and/or short personal notes regularly to friends suffering illness or tragedy.

"They're not maudlin, but just to let them know that I'm thinking of them," she says. "I alternate between those that warm the heart and those that tickle the funny bone. Sometimes a good laugh is appreciated even by those going through the worst of times. We wish we could find a cure, but if that's not the case, there are alternatives that can let people know that they're in our thoughts."

One thing Sally has discovered for certain: "I don't believe in saying 'I know just how you feel,' because no one can know exactly how someone else feels at any level. And, I don't believe in avoidance of the situation. It's not easy to confront these difficult situations, but extending a listening ear or sharing a hug is often the most appreciated gift one can give and requires very little investment on the part of the giver."

Words to Live By

"Sometimes a good laugh is appreciated even by those going through the worst of times. We wish we could find a cure, but if that's not the case, there are alternatives that can let people know that they're in our thoughts."

Be Brave, Be Strong, Mike
A Construction Worker Steps Up to Help a Young Boy Heal

Strong is the hand that lifts the soul.
—Kolpen, *The Secrets of Pistoulet*

The call to caring doesn't always come on the other end of a telephone—a relative phoning to say an elderly parent is hospitalized. Sometimes, it surprises—a human being, even a stranger, shows up on our path and the mystery and power of being open and giving to another unfolds. When we have empathy, we are living our openness. In this story, two lives cross accidentally. There is no great deed, but rather the response to a need. One man opened himself to the opportunity to befriend a sick little boy. The universe embraced that union. To be human means to be open to others.

Michael "Mike" Osting was in first grade and just beginning to make new buddies on the school playground when he was diagnosed with acute lymphocyte leukemia. For five months, doctors at the Children's Hospital of Philadelphia waged war against the grapefruit-sized tumors that had invaded his body and were growing fast.

But the then seven-year-old did what most kids often do: he found creative ways to stave off the day-to-day monotony of the sterile medical environment and the excruciating pain of his illness. His explorations led him to his hospital room window.

That was January 2001. That same month, Richard Ritchie, an iron worker from Philadelphia, was starting a new job—construction of a new ten-story tower just outside Michael's third-floor window at the hospital.

Ritchie says he'll never forget his first day on the job. "I looked up and saw this kid with no hair and his face up to the window, and I just remember thinking something about him was very special," says the father of three. "I just kept thinking, that poor little kid, he must be really, really sick. I waved and he smiled this huge smile and waved back."

Throughout the winter and spring, one thing remained constant: Mike standing at the window watching as 3,000 tons of steel were erected. Soon, he began coloring signs and holding up these messages to Ritchie and the dozens of workers on his crew. "Hi Local Iron Workers 401. I'm Mike." And, the construction crew started writing back.

Mom Cindy Osting recalls one exceptionally trying day when Mike was crying out in pain caused by the feeding tube crammed into his stomach. "I looked out the window at that blue construction crane and there were about two dozen guys standing on the scaffolding holding a sign: 'Be Strong Mike.'" She burst into tears. "Mike was so brave, but it was so hard on him. But then every day, these guys in hard hats would be there waving at him and cheering him on." Then there was the day when the third floor was constructed and Ritchie jumped across between the buildings and tapped on Mike's window, and the two had a window-side chat.

The friendship became the buzz of the hospital. And, as the ten floors of the building stacked up, so did the numbers of window-side viewers. Hospital administrators embraced the friendships. They forged official ties by staging construction worker-led tours of the new facility for the kids; holding a construction worker "signing" of the steel trusses (the crews spray-painted the names of Mike and dozens of kids on the steel trusses with the message "Get well"); and forming an official design committee for the children so they could share their input on design for the 146 private rooms under construction for the new tower.

"The irony is we were trying to do everything we could to minimize the stress of the construction on the children, and then we see them all there plastered to their windows and fascinated by the whole process," says John McDonough, vice president for Children's Hospital.

The result of patient-inspired construction ideas: today, new rooms all have DVD players, computer hook-ups, and laminated walls so the kids can bring in their own posters to decorate. Sleeper sofas for parents are in every room. Cafeterias are located on floors far away from patient rooms, so children nauseous from chemotherapy don't have to smell meals being cooked; phones are located just outside patient rooms so parents can call other family members away from the ears of anxious patients; and playrooms for siblings are on every floor.

Ritchie says Mike "changed the course of my life. Let's just say I was a real hard-core guy with not a lot of compassion. But, I'd look forward to seeing this kid every day waving at me and smiling and excited about our construction. I realized anything can happen to you at any time and I look at life completely differently thanks to him."

Today, Mike is a twelve-year-old fifth grader in complete remission from the cancer. "I'm going to be a construction worker when I grow up," he says.

Words to Live By

"Mike changed the course of my life. Let's just say I was a real hard-core guy with not a lot of compassion. But, I'd look forward to seeing this kid every day waving at me and smiling and excited about our construction. I realized anything can happen to you at any time and I look at life completely differently thanks to him."

The Call to Help Strangers
Entrepreneur Embraces the Opportunity to Serve

Every day in our lives has brought us to exactly where we are. When we don't already know what is calling us to act, all we need to do is listen right where we are—it will probably be near. Wherever you are, whatever you are doing, you can serve there.
—Ram Dass

Imagining yourself in someone else's shoes is the heart and soul of caregiving. Mary Ellen Hogan has never had cancer. In fact, this forty-something mom of two is a poster girl for healthy living, fitness, and wellness. But, Mary Ellen has come to know that one of the most common things people with cancer and chronic illness can feel is being terribly alone. When the c-word kept intruding in her life because of the illnesses of those around her, Mary Ellen asked herself, "How would I feel if I were the patient?" Then, she asked herself how she could cultivate compassion and came up with some small acts, right at her fingertips, that might help improve the mood and happiness of those experiencing the isolation of hospitalization and treatment.

For the past five years or so, Mary Ellen has become a culinary chaplain of sorts, a kitchen crusader for the sick, feeding body and soul.

As owner of Urban Harvest, a gourmet shop in downtown Arlington Heights, Illinois, just blocks from Northwest Community Hospital, she runs a burgeoning business for the close friends, family, and colleagues of hospital patients who stop in her store looking for a recipe for comfort. They seem to find it in soothing food.

"I want to bring a warm meal, something that will make her feel nurtured," is a collective request she hears regularly from customers en route to and from the hospital and adjacent long-term care center. "They stop in here, they tell me their stories, some cry a little and I listen. It happens a lot. It's hard for them to reconcile and find meaning."

At the same time, her shop caters the "Mommy and Daddy Dinner Baskets" for the hospital's birthing center. She often ponders the irony in serving both the healthy and those seeking healing.

For the latter, she typically does all she can do. She sends them off with baskets brimming with tangy cheese dips, soups, chicken dishes, and desserts that melt in your mouth.

It all started one year at Thanksgiving. One of her customers came in and told Mary Ellen about another customer who was battling cancer. The customer asked to remain anonymous but asked the Urban Harvest chef and shop owner to create a feast to deliver to the woman and her family on Thanksgiving. The staff did exactly that, creating a smorgasbord of Thanksgiving treats, with flowers, candles, and all the trimmings.

"This angel didn't want the woman to worry about cooking," says Mary Ellen. "She knew that as a mom, the woman would feel so bad if she couldn't have her family over for Thanksgiving as she did every year."

This was a pivotal moment for the family, and for Mary Ellen. She learned later that the woman was able to have a wonderful last supper with her two daughters that year. She died just before Christmas.

Since then, Mary Ellen has helped dozens of customers make their caring visible through the comfort of food.

Most recently, Mary Ellen found herself confronted head-on with cancer and death through the grief of her twelve-year-old daughter. The daughter's best friend had lost her mother to breast cancer. Her daughter was distraught, and there didn't seem to be much she could do.

"It hit so close to home, watching this woman my age suffer through this and then die," says Mary Ellen. "How do you deal with this with your children? How can you make sense of it? I didn't know what to do, what to say to my daughter, what to say to the family."

So, she started packing up food—lots of it—to bring to the family after the funeral.

"My daughter was like, 'Mom, food? That's stupid. We need to do something more.' I told her that that is what people do, they bring food. The food symbolizes that you care and love the family. It's a way of offering strength and hope."

Words to Live By

"I told her that that is what people do, they bring food. Food symbolizes that you care and love the family. It's a way of offering strength and hope."

Tips for Being a Friend in Sickness and in Health

Make the first move. Common life experiences make for a great start for friendships—even if they are born out of adversity. These shared experiences often lead to lifelong friendship. Pick up the phone. Send an e-mail or write a note that says, "I care. I am here."

Just listen. When someone is ill, just being able to share his or her story with a compassionate listener can make all the difference in the world. Sometimes being a friend means just listening, just offering a shoulder to cry on.

Stay connected. Be aware of your friend's boundaries—they will give you subtle cues. So, if they don't want you to call at work and discuss their illness or ask friends about it or call late in the night, don't. But find out how they do feel comfortable staying connected and try to honor the experience in that way. Maybe it is just a daily e-mail to say you care.

Pay it forward. Friendships are often celebrated in circles. One of the residing themes we've heard from those suffering from terminal illness or cancer is "do unto others." Many feel the need to reach out to others to offer hope and healing.

→ Getting Started: The Inside Track on Carrying Each Other

Buy someone this book. Cultivating compassion for others doesn't have to be a monumental task or a life calling. Rather it is sometimes in the small acts of giving that we find ways of opening our hearts. If we look to our own skills and talents, we often find, like Mary Ellen Hogan did, the recipe for connecting to other people and being there for them when they need us most. As Krista Burke discovered, there is often a sixth sense in each of us that guides us to caring experiences that can make the most profound difference. Rich Ritchie, a Philly construction worker, looked up one day and saw a little boy with cancer who needed him. In simply making a friend and reaching out to the young boy, he says his life was changed forever. What gifts are waiting to unfold inside of you that can help someone else? Who needs you now?

Tips for Taking Care of the Caregiver

"This can be the most challenging, rewarding, heartbreaking, and beautiful of times," according to Kerstin Sjoquist, a licensed hypnotherapist and producer of the Bliss Trips CD collection.

"As a caregiver, especially if you are caring for someone where there is a strained relationship, your physical and emotional resilience will be tested," said Sjoquist. "Taking care of yourself may be a low priority in the light of other tasks, and it is often the last thing on most people's lists. However, if you're going to attend to someone else's needs quickly and efficiently—and with a good attitude—it's vital to care for yourself as well."

Tend to basic needs. It's difficult to care for a person in need if you yourself are run-down. Make sure to address your immediate needs for adequate rest and sound nutrition. Schedule in a few brief but potent breaks into your day. A short walk around the block helps, or a catnap can do wonders to refresh you. If you can't physically get away, you can literally take a "breather."

Blow off steam. Do something active each day—walking, running, biking, swimming—anything that gets you moving. Take time to get outside and out into the world—even if it's just taking a walk down the street and back—and pay attention to your surroundings. A regular mind/body practice can help you fight stress before it starts. Yoga, Pilates, qigong, and other mindful disciplines create greater flexibility and strength as well as a relaxed body and mind.

Ask for help. Being a caregiver is an extremely demanding task. Rather than becoming overwhelmed and ineffective, ask someone to share the load before it becomes unbearable. It may be as simple as having a friend pick something up at the grocery store.

From the CarePages Frontlines

You've Got Mail

"My sister had breast cancer three years ago, and though she now suffers from lymphodema, she is doing great. Last February I was diagnosed with breast cancer too. The best part of every day was "mail call"! Real mail. I received cards nearly every day of my treatments, and it was a lifesaver. Some cards showed concern, others were *soooooo* funny. The gift of laughter was something I'll cherish forever. If you can't think of anything else to do, send cards. I'll never forget the lesson I learned from it. By the way, I'm doing great too."
—*Eve Gilmore*

Tell Her What Makes Her Special

"For anyone going through this, it helps to remind her what makes her special; whether it's a sense of humor, or she's a great listener, thoughtful of others, inspiring, or sharing some favorite music—any quality that makes her unique and important to you. Let her know how appreciated she is and reassure her, however this illness affects her, she is still that same special *person* at heart."
—*Krista Kretschmer*

Nine-to-Five Help Is On Its Way

"When my friend was diagnosed with breast cancer, her coworkers donated some of their vacation time to her. She worked in a large office, and each employee donated one day of their vacation time to her to use for surgery, chemo, radiation, or however she chose to use it. That way, she didn't have to go with any unpaid time off during her sick leave and she still had some time to take off for herself during the year. That is one way to do something without having to say, 'What can I do for you?' and it's really appreciated."
—*Becky Rammes*

Laughter Is the Best Medicine

"A friend of mine who had breast cancer shared a special idea with me that she found helpful during her treatments. Her friends all contributed a monetary donation and then went to area restaurants and got gift certificates. She also received a menu from each of the restaurants so that they could plan to dine in or take out. She said that her appetite was not the best so she could pick soup while her husband could eat a hearty meal. They also put the menus in a Tupperware container with a poem. The poem talked about how people don't want to eat their own food so why should she. It made her laugh. I have recently done this for a friend that has lung cancer and she also loved it."

—*Karla Primrose*

CHAPTER 7

As Time Moves On

The Heart and Soul of the Healing Process

I am not dying, not anymore than any of us are at
any moment. We can run, hopefully as fast as we
can, and then everyone must stop. We can only
choose how we handle the race.
— Hugh Elliott

Facing the fact that our loved one isn't going to get well, isn't
going to recover, or has died can point us in a new direction.
Suddenly, we are propelled into the emotional and the spiritual
practices of mystery.

How we navigate our own emotional health through our loved one's impending death and the final loss forces us to deal with complex factors that can influence our own health and well-being and our relationships at home, at work, and in the larger world.

The devastation surrounding terminal illness and loss can bind us in grief. Jim Warda, a father of three who recently lost both his parents, explains it best.

"After my mother died, a phrase came to me that helped me understand grief a bit more," says Jim. "We grieve to the depth we loved."

Sharing the journey of terminal illness and loss with someone we love can become part of a larger exploration into ourselves. When we walk through and with the experience with some else, if we are open to the experience, we will be taught the spiritual lessons of acceptance, letting go of the outcome, grace, and hope.

Here we explore stories that illustrate how companioning a loved one through illness and dying can become a healing process for ourselves. Perhaps what those of us who become caregivers on an emotional level for a loved one need to keep in mind is to be compassionate with ourselves, because it is a heartbreaking road to travel. The kindness and caring we extend to another is a gift we need to wrap around ourselves.

Sister Act

Daughters Step In to Care for a Dying Father
By Terry Gamble

Beth could not reason upon or explain the faith that gave her courage and patience to give up life, and cheerfully wait for death. Like a confiding child, she asked no questions, but left everything to God and nature, Father and Mother of us all, feeling sure that they, and they only could teach and strengthen heart and spirit for this life and the life to come.

—Louisa May Alcott, *Little Women*

Being present for a loved one who is dying is one of the most difficult challenges most of us will ever face. At a time when we want to give the deepest comfort, we often struggle to find just the right words to say and the gestures of compassion that will make a difference. Here, a daughter shares how, during her father's death, she and her sister learned that even though their father would be gone, a part of him will always be with them. In the end, the way he lived and the way he died will always nurture their lives.

It took my gynecologist to impress upon me that my father was dying. Digressing from the usual chatter about hormones and Pap smears, I spent the appointment talking about my *father's* condition, reciting the litany of illnesses, starting with the hospitalization for flu, the nausea, the terrible headaches, the pain in his hip, the little stroke, the gradual decline into invalidism, the falls, the fractured bone, the taking to his bed.

"He's dying," said my doctor.

And for the first time in months, I felt relieved. She'd hit the nail on the head. We'd been behaving as if my father's mortality was an affront, a failure in some essential way. Like an oak that was there before and presumably would be there long after we'd gone, he was a key figure in our landscape. If there were little signs of frailty along the way (a sore knee, a grimace, a dodgy hip), they were easy to ignore. We knew he was human; we just wouldn't accept the inevitable.

It was New Year's Eve 2002 when he first got sick. When he was first hospitalized, I caught a plane to Southern California. The first time you see a parent—especially one so stoic, so vibrant—stricken and gray, it stuns you. How could he have grown so old so fast?

I remember him sitting on the bed in his boxers and hospital gown, his wispy hair awry, his skinny bowed legs hanging over the edge. "Well," he said. "Well." He started to laugh as if he found the whole thing ridiculous. Then he told me to retrieve a black binder from his office, the one with his will in it.

My father was, at times, a difficult man. A stubborn man. An opinionated man. He was also, to my mind, a noble man. He felt it was his duty—his calling, even—to care for others. Thus he assumed the role as protector and provider and often as arbiter. Everyone turned to him, and he repaid our confidence by presiding with assuredness. For the better part of his adult life, he had sat on or presided over the boards of two hospitals, not to mention a number of schools and colleges and other civic organizations. If someone had a need, he responded.

But now he was tired. Besieged by physical limitations, he was bumping up against an even greater hurdle: the sinking realization of his wife's dementia. Nothing—not even my mother's stroke seven years earlier—prepared him for the challenge, the frustration, and the heartbreak of watching a loved one lose his or her mind.

"Helpless" was a foreign concept to my father. He had a Bronze Star for braving enemy fire as a communications officer during the Battle of the Bulge; he had a wall full of plaques commending him for his leadership in civic life. But neither courage nor authority was of any use in combating the fact of his wife's dying brain.

I retrieved the black binder containing the will as instructed by my father. When he came home from the hospital, we sat down with his wife, Helen. At my father's request (even though he wasn't dying; he couldn't be dying, could he?), I read his will. In typical fashion, it started with a joke. In a preamble to the legal jargon, the document read, "If anyone is fool enough to want my organs, they're welcome to them." I glanced at Helen. She stared vacantly at her hands. I cleared my throat. After all, it was mostly on her behalf that this reading was taking place. My father wanted to be sure that she knew if "something" happened to him, she would be cared for. And yet Helen didn't seem interested. In fact, she fell asleep.

That's when I knew something was really, really wrong.

Caretakers of people with Alzheimer's or dementia often become sick due to stress and lack of self-care. In the months that followed, my father was hospitalized again and again. There was a little stroke, a fall, an infection. And always—the pain. I sat by his bedside, and he—the leader, the hero—opened up. We talked about his second marriage, his despair. We talked about my mother. We talked about what to do next.

My sister and I, determined to get him well, took charge. It was no small feat wresting control away from a man who'd always held the tiller. He couldn't stay in the hospital and, sadly, he couldn't go home. We told our father, firmly and with the aid of a counselor from the Alzheimer's Association, that he had to let go.

All his life, our father had lived with other people. He went from college into the army, from the army into marriage. The brief interlude between my mother's death and his subsequent remarriage barely counted, and, as he pointed out, he'd never set up a home just for himself. "We are competent people," my sister and I told our father. I don't think he believed us. We were still, at forty-seven and fifty, his little girls. Overriding him, we set up an apartment right across from his office, arranged for a live-in nurse, and decorated it in a pleasant if utilitarian fashion. "When you get stronger," we told him cheerily, "you'll be able to ride on your scooter over to your office." He had capitulated to the scooter about six months earlier when it became clear that he would no longer be able to walk. The source of his pain was mysterious. Only later did an X-ray discover he'd been trying for months to navigate on a fractured hip.

Our cheery scenario, however, was not to be. He deteriorated. The pain was excruciating, so the doctors prescribed serious pain medication that dulled him. Failing further, he slipped into depression. His nurse confided that he was becoming difficult and morbid, that he was drinking too much alcohol as well as taking OxyContin. Watching him in that bed, seeing how trapped and hopeless he felt, I could only feel compassion. It was soon after that I spoke with my gynecologist.

Sometime around the beginning of 2004, my father went back into the hospital for more tests and, possibly, an attempt at a hip replacement, even though there was a good chance he wouldn't survive the surgery. Once in the hospital, however, the various scans showed cancer masses that had reappeared after a long-dormant bout of prostate cancer. The surgeon candidly informed us that he was clearly terminally ill. Still in denial, I blurted out, "*How* terminal?"

The months that followed were a blur of plane flights. I kept a nightgown and a set of clothes at my sister's house. We had a routine where I'd come so she could get some respite. Even at that, even with our dad's extraordinary VIP status at the hospital, my sister and I learned how much you have to advocate on the part of a patient. Just getting the docs to talk straight was challenging, as if they were embarrassed by our directness.

When we finally got answers, we interpreted and relayed them back to our father. We said, "If you get pneumonia, do you want us to treat you? If we don't treat you, you will die." He thought about this for a long time. He said, "This is no quality of life." Then he said, "I just don't want to end up gasping like a fish."

Deathwatches have a way of distilling and shrinking the world. I clearly remember, for instance, the pattern of the hospital carpet. Or going to a department store to buy cosmetics and thinking how foreign and unseemly the errand felt. Then there was the evening my father's wife came to the hospital in her wheelchair. She had been calling people for days, telling them he had already died. When her nurse said he hadn't died, she demanded to see him, even though he didn't want her to see him like that. Helen came anyway and sat by his bed and held his hand and wept.

It wasn't always grim. One evening, in the midst of weeping, he said, "This reminds me of the first poem I ever wrote."

"What poem, Dad?" I asked, also in tears.

"Dribble, dribble, little drop. How I wonder where you plop."

On the day he died, I arrived at his hospital room. His eyes were fixed, and he was drawing the gasping breaths he so dreaded. For a long time, I sat with him. We are not a religious family. We don't talk much about dying or where we go when we're gone. I think my father's beliefs were pantheistic; he embraced the notion that we are absorbed back into the divine circle of life. Did he think he'd see my mother again? His own parents and deceased siblings? We never talked about it, but my guess is no.

On the last day of his life, my father reached out to his five-month-old great granddaughter and touched her hand. When I arrived, the young woman who sat with him when we weren't there was reading to him from Revelation. I wanted to say, "He's not a believer," but looking at him, I could see it wasn't doing any harm. Besides, it seemed to comfort her. When I took her place, I told him I loved him and thanked him for all he'd done for us and told him not to worry, that we would be okay. After that, my sister came and told me that we should go home and get some sleep.

People who die slowly have the luxury of waiting for their family to gather before they go. My mother was like that. We were all there to watch her last breath. My father, on the other hand, always wanted to be in control. Around 3:00 A.M., my sister woke me. "That was the hospital," she said. "He's gone."

I will always have mixed feelings about not being there at the actual moment. It feels like abandonment. But this was a man who would barely let us care for him, so perhaps he preferred it this way.

That night, as I was returning to sleep, my father came to me, crystal clear and tangible. Instead of an eighty-one-year-old with a pain-ridden, broken body, he was thirty-one, vibrant and healthy. A huge smile on his face, he took my sister's and my hands. He said, "I just want to tell you that everything is fine, and this was absolutely the right thing to do. I . . . feel . . . great!"

Words to Live By

"I will always have mixed feelings about not being there at the actual moment. It feels like abandonment. But this was a man who would barely let us care for him, so perhaps he preferred it this way."

The hero, the leader, the uber-grownup was gone. Gradually I discovered that on the other side of the loss is something else: liberation, perhaps. Complete permission to be oneself.

Nevertheless, I still miss him. In his summer cottage in northern Michigan, I can't bring myself to tape over the outgoing message on the answering machine recorded in his voice. It's been almost three years.

Footprints in the Sandals
In Life and in Death, He Carried Us

There are times when silence is the most sacred of responses.
—Eugene Kennedy

Grief creates another kind of community. This story is about Mary Beth's teenage son, Thomas, and her next-door neighbor, Vince. It is the story that I believe brings home for all of us the precious idea that our humanity and the impact we've had on another person's life lives on long after we do. Sometimes, the only way we can say thank you to someone who has tremendously influenced our lives is to find a way to make sense of the mystery for ourselves and walk on, silently knowing we are carrying a part of their soul.

I found them yesterday—the Birkenstock sandals—during my weekly pre-straightening, cleaning patrol of my kid's rooms. They were buried under a clump of damp towels in my son Thomas's closet.

Immediately, memories of Vince flashed before me. This weekend is the one-year anniversary of the day he died. How his old, battered, favorite pair of shoes ended up in Thomas's closet is a story in itself.

But, in every way, yesterday I was avoiding thinking about the anniversary. I closed the closet door, pushed the memories aside, and raced out the front door to meet my Saturday morning running group. I hated and loved this 6:30 A.M. lapping-the-forest ritual. Yesterday, I couldn't wait to endure it.

Just when I hit the "I-am-not-a-runner-why-am-I-doing-this-wall," John Mayer's tune comes blasting through my MP3 player, the whole "Something's better outside the lines" mantra and the refrain about being "in-vince-ible."

I ran faster.

These days, I'm running because a year ago I didn't run. But the "invincible" Vince died unexpectedly in his sleep at age fifty-one after hosting a barbeque. Now, I am doing all the "I don't do that's" with an urgency.

Vince and his wife Helene and son Matt had become family.

Vince was the first hand that reached across the fence to welcome me and my family to the neighborhood sixteen years ago. Then, Thomas arrived in our lives, literally almost jumping out of his crib and his bedroom window at age two to bolt into their backyard; soon, he would become the much-welcomed sidekick to the Vince-and-Matt team. But Thomas never felt like a fence hopper as he played catcher, runner, and homerun hitter in the backyard games. We vacationed, hosted *Survivor* TV-watching parties, and celebrated all our holidays together. I love to cook, so I made meals and shared. Vince loved to take the boys on adventures, so Thomas traveled to Wrigley Field, fishing holes, and other places that became etched in his heart forever.

When my family was no longer a two-parent-in-the-same-house unit, Vince and Helene were the glue that held us together, always. Vince was the guy who waved and casually called over *every* day when my son Thomas was going through a difficult time: "How is he doing?" And the guy who took Thomas aside, patted him on the back, and said, "Hey buddy, you're going to be okay." When people say it takes a village to raise a child, they paid tribute to Vince and Helene and the "family" they had become.

At the wake, hundreds of people poured in to say good-bye to Vince. Many to this day remark or remember the neighbor "son-almost Matt's brother" in the corner: Thomas, hunched over and sobbing uncontrollably over the loss of a man who had loved him unconditionally, a man who opened his heart in such a big way for many years. I have never felt as sad as a year ago today, when I had to tell Thomas that Vince had died. He looked at me and pleaded: "Mom, Mr. Gillespie can't die."

It should be no surprise to find the shoes buried in Thomas's closet. Ironically, they came into our house during the New Orleans Katrina crisis, when I was helping a group collect "Soles" for people who didn't have shoes. After his death, Helene donated all of Vince's shoes, and I remember looking at the Birkenstocks with Helene and laughing about Vince's whole post-hippie fascination, the tie-dyed shirts he started making after our joint family trip to San Francisco, and the shoes he wore every day.

I remember Thomas picking one up. "Those shoes are so Mr. G," he said. I also remember that the day after Vince's funeral was the epiphany moment, the turning point when Thomas abruptly changed direction and headed back to the boy who laughed his head off riding around Sanibel Island in a rented convertible with Vince and Matt during our annual June vacations.

A part of me knows that Vince is watching over Thomas now in a way that only someone who understands the shoes can appreciate. Thomas gets it. Vince carried him in his life and he saved him in his death.

This week a group of our friends—me, Helene, some of Vince's high school friends—went to Ravinia, and we celebrated the time that we all got to walk alongside Vince in life. We laughed. We cried. And we tried to hold on to the memories of the one missing from the circle.

In some ways, Thomas holds the secret to moving on in his closet. There, he has found a way to step into the footprints of the man who carried him through many of his happiest times and his hardest struggle. Vince stepped out in life with great style and class. I hope someday that Thomas tries on the shoes.

Words to Live By

"We celebrated the time we all got to walk alongside Vince in life. We laughed. We cried. And we tried to hold on to the memories of the one missing from the circle."

Finding the Life in Loss

Creating Customized "Celebrate the Memories" Ceremonies
By Paul Von Driska

Those who are dead are never gone.
—Joan Halifax

Most religions have funeral rites, spiritual practices, or rituals for saying good-bye. They are designed to provide connection and the understanding that we are not alone and to help us through the initial stages of our deep sorrow. Here, Paul, an executive from Wales, shares how the creative rituals to honor someone that his friends and family members have created inspired his final tribute to a friend, Rick, who died suddenly of cancer.

The first time I attended a funeral where friends and family members spoke was in 1988 in Tennessee. It was my neighbor and work associate's brother, who was only in his forties. The last friend spoke about how Dave's brother had a habit after they had all been out at a bar socializing for the evening, and he decided to leave, he would "sneak out" without saying good-bye. He concluded by saying, "I guess he's snuck out on us for good this time."

So when our neighbor Rick died, I went back for the funeral, and I wanted to say some things about him. I got in late the night before and drove to his and Jan's house that morning. It was hard to go to the door not knowing how she'd be and whether she'd have time for me. She was very glad to see me. We talked. Mostly she did, about the last week, how tough he was, how much pain, how she couldn't give him his wish to die at home because he deteriorated so quickly. I asked if I could say a few words at the funeral and she was delighted. One of his work associates also had arranged to say a few words. It was a combined wake and funeral; he was well liked by people at all levels in the company, so there were hundreds of people there. The priest went through a short service, then spoke about Rick's history and family and did an excellent job.

Words to Live By

"We talked. Mostly she did, about the last week, how tough he was, how much pain, how she couldn't give him his wish to die at home because he deteriorated so quickly."

Then I told several stories about Rick, the great neighbor, dog lover, golfer, and hard-working father. His coworker had a lot of excellent stories of Rick the proud father as his daughters were growing up.

I think it meant a lot to Jan and her girls to hear other people saying what a great husband and dad they had. Sometimes we carry each other by reminding loved ones of how they carried us.

♥ From the CarePages Frontlines

Laughter Lightens the Load

"My mother is recovering from a lumpectomy. My parents live on the opposite coast from me so when I found out about her cancer I scheduled a two-week trip to visit. The hospital she is being treated at is an hour away and my parents are both in their eighties. When I drove them to appointments my dad frequently joked with the doctors and nurses. They seemed surprised that someone would be able to joke and laugh. One day while sitting in the oncology waiting room, my dad made a joke and we both laughed. Everyone in the waiting room looked at us and smiled. It really seemed to lighten the whole room. Even when dealing with cancer it is important to find things to laugh about and ways to continue to enjoy life. It was great for both my parents and me to have those weeks together at that time. I was able to do a lot of work around their house that they really appreciated too."

—Marie Campbell

Creating a Lifetime of Memories

"My mother has cancer. To help her I asked friends, family, coworkers, anyone I could think of, to share a memory with me of my mom. Sometimes it was very difficult to get people to share, but once you started them thinking, it got easier. I typed and edited these "memories" on little slips of colored paper, using first-person style so it sounded like the person who gave the memory was speaking directly to my mom. I folded the memories and placed them in an apothecary jar that I had decorated with lace and a little poem. I presented it to Mom on Mother's Day with the intention of her looking at one memory a day to help keep her positive. Of course, that didn't work. She wanted to read all of them at once, and we had the most precious time sharing them. We laughed, we cried, we got sentimental, and I felt closer to my mom that day than I had for a long time. She tells me that she reads these memories over and over and over again and that it was the best gift she ever received. It didn't cost anything . . . just some time. I encourage anyone who wants to do something really special to try it. I think it's a no-fail way to lift someone's spirits."

— *Tamara Fisher*

CHAPTER 8

CARING FOR THE CAREGIVER

Healing and Pain Are Powerful, Transformative Teachers

Illness offers an extraordinary and at times
frightening vantage point from which to view
the terrain of one's life.
—Kat Duff

When we care for someone else, we get a glimpse of our own being. When we show up at someone's hospital bedside, when we sit in a park to listen as a friend cries over the suffering her son is experiencing in the hospital and how frustrated she is, when we're just there with people, something inside us shifts too. When we share another person's pain, we're reminded of who we really are and are recharged with an urgency to make the most out of the time we have here and what we have to offer others.

There is a tremendous value in being of service to others. But when we are the source of comfort for another, sometimes those we help turn out to be healers for us. When Gandhi was asked why he served the poor, he said, "I am here to serve no one else but myself, to find my own self-realization through the service of these village folk." As Gandhi suggests, even when we are helping others, we are working on ourselves, and every act of compassion has a ripple effect on us. We also must realize that we can only attend to others if we have been compassionate to ourselves. Healing energy is available for others only when we are our own caregivers first.

"The most important thing a caregiver needs to do is make a conscious choice to be in it all the way," says Suzanne Mintz, director and president of the National Family Caregivers Association. "Even if you know taking care of someone else is going to be tremendously stressful, even if the relationship is strained, you don't have the time, or it is too emotionally draining, you have to make the commitment to yourself and the other person to be in it 100 percent. When you do, both of you begin the healing."

A Caring Gesture from the Cutting Edge

I weep your tears—pour them onto me my child.
—Karl Rahner

When Jake Jacobson wrote to us at CarePages, he had no idea that what he was calling a "simple gesture" for a friend's loved one speaks volumes about what it means to carry each other and to act, even though we have no idea what to do or say.

What happened in a tiny urban Utah fire department is a lesson we can all take as an inspiration to get involved, to act.

Last summer, when one of the firefighter's wives was stricken with cancer, Jake says the firefighters would listen to their comrade describe all the stages, and they felt helpless hearing about how this guy's wife was going through things like hair loss and having to shave her head. One day, the firefighter showed up with a pair of clippers and asked another guy to shave his head in support of his wife.

Jake recalls, "After he explained to the crew why he was shaving his head, other members volunteered to show their support by shaving their heads too. Word spread to the station, and there, even more members followed suit. In the following days other members of the department did the same. Some of these firefighters were new members and had never met this woman before, but they willingly did this to show support not only for her but for their fellow firefighter also.

"While I never personally heard how much she appreciated this, I do know how it affected my crewmate. While this is evidence of the camaraderie that causes firefighters to refer to one another as 'brothers,' I hope it can also be an example to those who may have loved ones and friends touched by cancer and other devastating illnesses and conditions," says Jake.

Words to Live By

"Some of these firefighters were new members, and had never met this woman before, but they willingly did this to show support not only for her but for their fellow firefighter also."

No question, these guys think what they did is a small gesture, but they are role models for all of us about how the seemingly small things can make a huge difference in showing our support and caring for another.

The Reluctant Caregiver
When Relationships Are Strained, Caregiving Can Be Extra Tough

I believe in the power of hope, because I have seen people survive in ways that astound me.
—Joyce Rupp

A part of caregiving that rarely is addressed is how difficult it is. Many of us are great at caring for everyone else. But we forget to have compassion for ourselves. It is only in giving to ourselves that we can reach out and take care of others. These stories hint at the emotional and spiritual landmines a growing number of people face when they suddenly and unexpectedly are thrown into the role of caregiver.

After years of coping with the emotionally charged and excruciatingly painful divorce of her parents, it came time for the adult daughter to assume the care of her aging mom and dad. The lifelong irreconcilable differences were compounded by incompatible distances—her folks lived hours away from each other. She found herself running ragged from one parent's house to the other, struggling to take care of them, and having to listen to and endure their ongoing battle.

"She said, 'They were never there for me when I needed them because they were always fighting with each other, and now I'm supposed to take care of them?'" recalls Roberta Cole, coauthor of *Caregiving from the Heart: Tales of Inspiration.*

This woman's plight underscores what is happening in hundreds of homes where people who had strained relationships with their elderly parents are called on to pick up the around-the-clock caregiving.

The woman told Cole, "I'm resigned to doing this because when they're not around, I'll feel guilty. It's just sad to see they never are going to stop hating each other."

Cole recounts how another man told the story of his estranged relationship with his father. He is gay, and his father rejected him when he was a young adult. Now, years later, his father's health was failing, and he was the only one who showed up at his dad's bedside.

"He came back to care for his father, because he felt it was his last hope to melt the ice," says Cole, a New York City writer and university teacher who took care of her own mother during her last ten years. "He was hoping that finally he could find a way for his dad to identify with him and to share a bond they never had."

"Even if you had the best parent in the world, every caregiver is at some point reluctant or at least ambivalent, making the difficulty of the situation even greater," says Cole.

Taking on the role of caretaker can be especially tough for adult children who may have to navigate caring for an elderly parent who wasn't that great at parenting. Or, with the growing divorce rate and evolving scope of families, many ex-spouses are finding themselves thrust into the role of caregiver for their children's father or mother—the person they divorced. Also prevalent are those people who are forced to take on the role of caretaker in very nonloving and often abusive relationships.

Illness becomes a spiritual teacher in the practices of forgiveness, prayer, and letting go, according to Amy Baker, a self-proclaimed "reluctant caregiver," who chronicles her perseverance and hope as she coped with the decline and death of her parents in her book, *Slow Dancing at Death's Door: Helping Your Parents through the Last Stages of Life.* The book details Baker's own strained relationship with her parents and how she reconnected with both of them before their deaths.

"Dealing with the emotional and spiritual issues becomes paramount," says Baker, a Fort Worth, Texas, mom of two teenagers. "The raw emotions just come pouring out. What we don't realize is that all of these unresolved relationships are simmering somewhere ready to surface. The reality is, we all will become sick and die one day, and our loved ones will too. It's a truth we can no longer ignore."

Indeed, this reluctant caregiver dilemma is positioned to spread as our population is living longer. The nation's largest demographic—78.2 million Baby Boomers—increasingly face caring for aging parents, their own mortality and need for health care, along with the care of their children, friends, and coworkers. According to a 2005 study by Campbell-Ewald Health, 13 million Baby Boomers are currently caregivers for their aged parents. This year, the oldest of the generation born between 1946 and 1964 will turn sixty years old.

"The luckiest ones are able to focus on the patient and not all the issues with their parents, but that's rare," says Baker. "Most of the time, you're going to face some pretty heavy spiritual and emotional baggage through the experience of caregiving."

Even when we're able to overcome our misgivings and provide care for an elderly relative or loved one with whom the loving was not so visible, the reluctant caregiver syndrome spills over to the sibling front, where family members are stuck repeating childhood conflicts and having those conflicts turn into a war over how to best care for Mom and Dad, according to Kevin O'Connor, a professional speaker, consultant, and pastoral counselor and educator at Loyola University in Chicago.

What's more, caregivers of parents, ex-spouses, or relatives who haven't been loving or caring can feel especially alone and isolated, said Lori Ovitz, whose personal story was introduced on page 117. Through her nonprofit organization—*www.facingthemirror.org*—this Hollywood and TV makeup artist visits patients—adults, teens, and children—at the University of Chicago Hospitals and across the country, using makeup to make a difference in how cancer patients and their caregivers look and feel.

Frequently, Ovitz deals with young children whose parents are "overwhelmed by what has happened to their child and just can't deal with it."

"They do their best to be the caregiver, but the role is too overwhelming," said Ovitz. "There was one little baby boy for whom everyone decided it was just better to stay in the hospital and be cared for than to go home. It's heartbreaking."

For all caregivers—unexpected, reluctant, no matter what the situation—caregiving is a role that is learned along the way.

"We learn that caregivers come in many different forms, that there is no right way to care, and that if we can take care as well as give it and make peace with the experiences along the way—it can be a transformative journey," says Cole.

Tips for Caring for a Difficult Parent or Family Member

+ Give yourself permission to be angry or resentful about your caregiving role, according to Cole. "The only way you are going to work things through is to acknowledge that those are feelings you have a right to feel," said Cole. "But then you also have to realize that it is not going to change and that you either have to work through the anger and get to the other side or you are going to have a terrible struggle."

+ Baker stresses the need for "getting angry and getting over it." You can do this, in part, by learning how to separate the past from the present in dealing with a strained parent-child relationship.

+ Try not to merge the past with the future, says Baker.

+ Treat your resentment and anger about the lack of a loving relationship with compassion—for yourself and for the person you are caring for. "As hard as it is to do, realize that most people are only doing the best they can," says Baker. "Their meanness or lack of love for you probably wasn't malicious. They didn't set out to hurt you and now is a good time to practice forgiveness."

+ Letting go can be transforming for you, adds Baker.

+ Don't be afraid to seek help from a third party—another relative, a friend, a former professional associate of your parent, or an elder care professional—if you're feeling overwhelmed trying to care for a difficult parent, says Cole.

+ Sometimes when the situation is so painful and you've tried everything to heal the pain, the only thing you can do is turn to God's grace, recommends Baker.

Tips for Creating a Caring Community of Siblings: Sidelining Sibling Rivalry
By Kevin E. O'Connor, CSP, Loyola University in Chicago

1. *Prioritize.* Speak the priority of the day, week, or hour. Work to agree on these priorities. What is most important for our suffering parent now? This will help each member of the family to decide how they will then act. This is especially helpful with legal and financial issues. Not everything has to be decided upon tonight. But priorities do need to be enunciated.

Resources for Finding the Sacred in Caregiving

The following is a reading from "A Spiritual Director Reflects on Illness, Healing and Death," by Rita L. Petrusa OP, in *Journey's Companion,* a publication of Loyola University's Institute of Spiritual Leadership. It is a reflection on moving back into daily life as a patient, caregiver, or healer.

"Healing is different from curing. I have come to know that there are many levels on which healing can happen—emotional, spiritual, and mental and probably others. . . . Healing means . . . being able to hold all possible outcomes, living with the unknown and trusting the Ultimate Goodness—that even if my body dies, the essence of who I am is safe and will never die. I truly believe this."

Make priorities and attempt to agree. Then watch what happens next.

2. *Talk with respect.* Even if you don't normally get along, be respectful and kind and forgiving. If you act "as if" you feel that way, you will often actually feel that way, and it will look like you really feel that way! Be this way with physicians and staff as well. When you are respectful, they are likely to be also. This works even better on those who are a challenge to us and who at first are not very kind. "Kill 'em with kindness" does work.

    Work to be firm when you need to be. "Firm and friendly," Dr. Rudolf Dreikurs, the Chicago psychiatrist, used to say. Firmness shows respect for you, friendly shows respect for them.

Being respectful and kind in no way means being a pushover. It simply means you have a rule within yourself to speak clearly in a way that invites a response and not retaliation.

3. *Seek help.* Use the chaplain services that may be available, or at least use the chapel.

   Even the strongest among us needs a break from the action. Use the chapel or meditation room frequently just to get your thoughts together. And try inviting your younger brother, the feisty one, to come with you. Hold his hand and ask him to remember his fondest memory of Mom. See what happens next.

4. *Hold family meetings.* Set up regular family consultation meetings. Regular meetings will help in sharing news, progress, making decisions, and so on. It also allows for some camaraderie as well as some relaxing discussion. Emergency after emergency is bad enough, try not to make it a habit to plan in this way. Defer things if you can to a family meeting. "Let me talk to my siblings about that" is a great way to put some important time between you and someone else who wants a "now" decision. You can do these meetings online, over the phone, in person, over a meal — or all of the above.

5. *"What I liked best," "what I notice about," "it was helpful when," "I especially appreciate"* are all ways to communicate encouragement to others. They are also ways to train ourselves to focus on those aspects of warmth between ourselves and others. Just use some of these each day with siblings and staff, and then watch what happens next.

6. *Focus on progress.* It is very, very easy to focus on the back-sliding, emergencies, prescriptions, and relapses. Yes, these are real. But so is the way Dad looked at his grandchild that day, so is the squeeze Mom gave your hand, so is the funny story the nurse told us—all of these are just as real as the pain we see and the pain we are in. Notice what is happening in small and yet significant ways.

7. *Outsource disagreements.* When major disagreements occur, consider an outside expert, counselor, or pastor for help. Don't try to do everything yourself. You can hire any professional by the hour and give them the charge to "help us over this hump." An outsider can help siblings behave, focus, and decide in ways an older sister or brother never could. No one needs to change his or her personality. They just need to help Mom or Dad in their suffering. Specialists can help us focus.

8. *Create one-on-one time.* Take your brother to lunch, go to church with your born-again sister, babysit for the grand-kids, and take two siblings to the movies. One-on-one time is replete with subtle wonders if only you will take the initiative to do it. No big deal here, simply a genuine invitation.

    This works especially well with those we are estranged from. Our motorcycling sister from Utah, our brother who hasn't called in four years, that estranged ex-sister-in-law whom your mother loved and kept in touch with—all are worthy of some one-on-one time. Just act "as if" they were an interesting stranger and talk and listen and share and remember. Just don't try to change them and maybe they won't try to change you!

One-on-one time can also be those times when your parent is sleeping, you are bored or worried, and the hospital housekeeper is working in the room. Talk to her. Take an interest in her children, her career, her work. Don't interfere with her doing her job, but learn her name and the names of her children and remember them for tomorrow. Then watch what happens next!

9. *Call on hospice.* Reach out for help through hospice, ministry of care, and respite services that may be available.

   Fear grips us about hospice care—Mom must really be dying, some will think. Visiting ministers are strangers in our midst—what gives them the right? Respite service? You mean I can take time off and not feel guilty?

   These services are for us in this time of need, but mostly they are for our parent. We are better off, much better off, when we are rested; we can attend well to our own families, and understand the realities of the body and the disease.

   I have yet to meet a family who used hospice who is unhappy with the decision. There may be some, I just haven't met them. My own mom used them three times.

   Ministers of care are representatives of your parents' church, perhaps some of the most important "strangers" who will come into the room for an aging and dying person.

   Respite services, even neighbors who will come and sit while you rest, attend a school function, or play with your children (or your siblings) can help reinvigorate your world and your ultimate service to your parents.

10. *Celebrate.* Celebrate some together time, if only in the hospital cafeteria, through remembrances and memories of the past through pictures, statues, music, and movies.

My father's last night was a real Irish wake, and he was still alive to attend and enjoy it! As he lapsed in and out of consciousness and began to breathe heavier and heavier, my sister asked a few friends to be with her and dad with their fiddles, singing, and praying aloud. My father always had the old Catholic wish for a "happy death." Little did he know it would be accompanied by fiddles!

From the CarePages Frontlines

Form a Circle of Friends

"As a six-year breast cancer survivor, I can tell you that having a support group is half the battle of beating this disease. I was diagnosed at age twenty-six and that age is supposed to be the prime of your life. Instead, I was losing my hair, eyelashes, and going through something that no one should have to experience. My family and friends realized that they could not 'fix' this problem for me.

"They rallied around me, visited me, made me get out, even for just a little while to get some fresh air, change of scenery, etc. I too enjoyed receiving mail every day from friends and even people I didn't know who were praying for me and my speedy recovery. When I completed my therapies, my family threw a 'Survivor Party' and invited all of those who supported me through my ordeal. For those caregivers, be persistent in helping your loved one—whether it is bringing her food, taking her out for a walk, going to the movies, or buying her groceries. Patience but persistence!"
— *Schelly Tennant Marlatt*

CHAPTER 9

MAKING CARING VISIBLE TO THE WORLD

Ordinary People Who Have Made
an Extraordinary Difference

We are here to do, and through doing to learn; and through
learning to know; and through knowing to experience wonder;
and through wonder to attain wisdom; and through wisdom to
find simplicity; and through simplicity to give attention; and
through attention to see what needs to be done.
—Ben Hei Hei

In this chapter we shine the spotlight on ordinary people who
have surmounted their own pain, illness, and loss to give back
to others. We go to hospital bedsides, walk-a-thon finish lines,

and living rooms across the country to profile the heroes who are creating healing spaces for those coping with catastrophic illness and loss.

Passing On the Legacy

When His Father's Death Left Him Grief-Stricken,
One Son Created His Own Lasting Tribute
By Michael Shmarak

There is no greater gift of charity you
can give than helping a person die well.
—Buddhist teacher Sogyal Rinpoche

Grieving the death of a loved one is one of the most difficult experiences most of us will ever have. This story brings us into the moment when Chicago public relations executive Michael Shmarak designed his own mourning ritual to pay lasting tribute to his father—and at the same time, to reach out to help others celebrate his father's life.

My father, Kenneth Lawrence Shmarak, lost his battle with leukemia on June 5, 2005. When he died at the young age of seventy, a significant part of my life was torn away. I have been searching for ways to fill that void so that I can move forward as much as I can.

Dad always taught me never to feel sorry for myself, to always appreciate and embrace what you have in the form you have it. With his health care background (he worked in dentistry, health insurance companies, and public health programs in Michigan, New Jersey, Colorado, and Ohio), Dad always felt that everything he did should help someone else and at the same time open the eyes of other people who didn't know that problems even existed.

That is why, to heal and go on, I decided to do what my dad did best—give back to others. I decided to orchestrate an ongoing blood drive that would continue to pour life into others who were facing the leukemia battle he so heroically waged.

I started DRIVE 6.05 on June 5, 2006, the first anniversary of his death. I didn't want to give it a name that had Dad's name on it. I want to remember him and his name for the memories I have of him that have nothing to do with the disease and personal traumas he went through. Rather, the drive should be a reminder that if we could help people who are trying to find a cure to leukemia—whether it be my dad's type or any other one—then we are doing something to extend the lives of people.

An innovative, no-pressure, please-pass-this-on-to-a-friend e-mail/electronic campaign, I promise to donate $6.05 to the Leukemia & Lymphoma Society (LLS) of Chicago for every pint of blood you, your friends, or your family donate. So far, a significant number of people have let me know about their blood donations, and the LLS has received monetary donations through the link we provided in our electronic newsletter.

My dad's bout with leukemia was eighteen months long. He went through intense chemotherapy, and his body began to whittle away as a result of the cancer and the drugs. But you could see that his spirit was never going away. My father had one of the strongest wills of anyone I know or knew, and it may be why I can be such a stubborn person at times. The fruit doesn't fall far from the tree, and his wife (my mom, Sue), and Amy, my wife, would tell you that the trait is both blessing and curse.

When the cancer went into remission, we were happy, but still knew we had a fight ahead of us. Dad had a lot of restrictions on what he could do, but he didn't want to sit back and just die. He tried to lead as normal a life as he could because that is how he wanted to be.

But sometimes fate has a strange way of working—connecting the dots of life in a way that cannot be explained. The morning of January 13, 2005—the very same morning I was bringing Amy to the hospital for the birth of my daughter, as well as Dad's "half-birthday"—he called and told me that the leukemia was back, and worse than before. That night, Dad's granddaughter was born, and to this day it is obvious that Ella Jade is connected to her grandfather.

His final straw came when we tried getting him to the University of Texas at Austin to meet a doctor who was studying the exact type of leukemia that Dad had. When we learned that his blood levels were not high enough, Dad threw in the proverbial towel and flatly said, "I am ready to die now." I cannot tell you how deeply that stung me, but concurrently it made me want to hug my father for staying true to his core belief: stay true to who you are, embrace what and who you have, and let chips fall where they may.

The doctors let him travel from Detroit to Chicago to meet Ella a week or so after she was born. A snowstorm hit Chicago that day; it was a sign from above for Dad to spend the entire day with Ella. An extra bonus—he was able to come back to Chicago for Ella's baby naming.

Shortly before he passed, I got pretty drunk at a work event, probably to help me deal with how I was feeling about the possibility of losing my father. For whatever reason, I went up to my computer and wrote my father a thank you note for everything he ever did and taught me—for staying true to who he was, for how much I admired his courage, for having to spend nearly half of his life sick in one form or another (he had an ileostomy when he was in his mid-thirties), and for being a good parent. I wanted to make sure he knew how I felt, and so he could have some good memories to think about in his last days. That letter was read at his funeral; I was as close to my father as anyone, and I didn't feel comfortable letting anyone else eulogize him.

I started DRIVE 6.05 as a way to help me cope with his loss and to help the Leukemia & Lymphoma Society in one small but ongoing way. The need for blood doesn't take vacations or time off; it can happen to anyone, anywhere and at any time, so why should a one-off blood drive? —Visit Michael's CarePage ("Shmarak Blood Drive") at *www.CarePages.com*.

Words to Live By

"I want to remember him and his name for the memories I have of him that have nothing to do with the disease and personal traumas he went through. Rather, the drive should be a reminder that if we could help people who are trying to find a cure for leukemia . . . then we are doing something to extend the lives of people."

Wounded Healer Shines Hope and Inspiration into the Life of a Stranger
Connection Forms Life-Sustaining Friendship

When two people come together, an ancient circle closes between them. They also come to each other not with empty hands, but with hands full of gifts for each other. Often these gifts are wounded gifts; this awakens the dimension of healing within love. —John O'Donohue

Barry Adkins had recently completed "The Cincinnati Flying Pig Marathon," the third largest marathon in the country. The idea that he could have lung cancer never crossed his mind. He'd never taken a puff of a cigarette in his life, and he exercised daily. In fact, the forty-nine-year-old father of two, husband, and triathlete was just thinking about retiring in a couple of years from his lifelong career in government service, and specifically, the environmental protection arena. Ironically, he'd directed air quality control and noise pollution efforts in two of his posts.

Then, in spring 2006, he was diagnosed with lung cancer.

"I was totally shocked," he recalls. "I had no symptoms. I've always been very optimistic; I just don't ever let the negative get to me. But this time, I was really scared. I said to myself, 'You are going to beat this.' My friends' and family's response was overwhelming. They just rallied from all sides."

In an affirmation that was part prayer, part resolution, Barry says he pledged, "Bring on the miracle."

Across the country, Bonnie Addario, a grandmother and former CEO, could still hear those words reverberating in her heart and soul: "You have lung cancer." (Bonnie's story is introduced on page 85.)

Even today, a two-year survivor, she still recoils when she remembers the day she was told the news. But, when cancer didn't do what doctors predicted it could and would do, and she found herself celebrating her two-year survival mark, it hit her: "I needed to reach beyond me and help others. I needed to make sure something more was being done to fight lung cancer."

Learning about Barry through the CarePages' network, Bonnie picked up the phone and placed the call: "I have been there. I know you are afraid. I am here." They talked for hours, and hours, on many, many days.

Barry had found a close confidante in cancer. And Bonnie had found a way to shine the gentle light of her soul back onto a new friend who also shared the wound of lung cancer.

On April 20, 2006, Bonnie posted a request for "the miracle" and asked for the prayers to pour in on Barry's behalf. She posted the following message on her CarePage ("BonniesBreath") and also put out the plea on the Web site for her foundation:

"Through my foundation, and CarePages, I have met a wonderful man who has just been diagnosed with lung cancer. His name is Barry Adkins. He lives in Kentucky, is married, and has two beautiful daughters. . . . I would like to ask everyone that reads this CarePage to please think of Barry every day and send him all of your well wishes and prayers."

In the months that followed, Barry too would pay homage to this remarkable angel and friend—the miracle—who accidentally stepped into his life. In spring 2006, he wrote on his CarePage, "Also, received a call from my friend Bonnie from out in California! She is a lung cancer survivor for two years and is truly an amazing story and an inspiration."

These days, Barry, who recently finished his last round of chemotherapy, is becoming the friend reaching out to help another behind him.

"Since I learned I had cancer, I have done more living in the past few months than I have in my whole life," says Barry. "I'm surrounding myself with wonderful moments with family and friends and looking so forward to everything that lies ahead. I have been so blessed by the people I know and Bonnie who reached out to walk me through this."

Recently, Barry was the visitor at the hospital, stopping bedside and bringing an autographed baseball to a fourteen-year-old boy he knows who has a terminal illness. "It's my turn to give back now."

Words to Live By

"I have been there. I know you are afraid. I am here."

Turning Grief into Purpose

*I guess I'll just have to wait until they become dragonflies, too.
Then they'll understand what happened to me and where I went.
— Water Bugs and Dragonflies: Explaining Death to Young Children*

Two words: Changing lives.

That's the essential mission of the Kylie Jane Long Foundation, which was launched to comfort and care for the parents and families of children who are very sick, mostly with cancer.

"We want to make sure that these parents can be there for their sick children around the clock," says Elizabeth Long, whose daughter Kylie died in an Ohio hospital of a rare form of cancer three days after her first birthday on May 6, 2005. Kylie's parents' commitment to turn their grief into purpose is testimony of the power of the human spirit to transform grief and the lessons learned from loss into purpose.

These days, Elizabeth and her husband Jason are devoted to the challenge of helping other parents with sick children and the medical community to better understand their plight. Kylie's little brother Andrew was born two months after her death on August 5, 2005. The foundation's goal: to enhance the lives of pediatric patients, educating parents and medical staffs, and raising awareness of rare pediatric cancers.

Their commitment and passion is born out of Kylie's short but inspiring life.

Kylie was about six months old when Elizabeth and Jason had the first clue that something was wrong. On January 1, 2005, Kylie had a low-grade fever, and her parents detected a small bulge in her abdomen and believed she had a hernia. They brought her to the emergency room. During the course of the next month, and several trips to the emergency room, it became apparent that something was seriously wrong. At the end of January, after insisting they were not going to leave the hospital until they had an answer, Elizabeth and Jason were told the unthinkable: "Your baby has cancer." Kylie and Jason and Elizabeth spent the next five months at Rainbow Babies' and Children's Hospital. "We were determined to fight and beat this horrible disease," recalls Elizabeth.

Nicknamed "Sweat Pea," Kylie's luminous spirit continues to be omnipresent. For Elizabeth, dragonflies hold a special significance. Symbolizing that we are light and can reflect the light in powerful ways if we choose, they remind her of Kylie. In Kylie's honor and to commemorate what would have been her birthday and the anniversary three days later of her passing, Andrew, Jason, and Elizabeth planted a backyard "dragonfly garden." Now, these light-makers buzz around as Andrew chases them. The walls of their home are decorated with dragonflies, and they hang from windows throughout the Long household, constant reminders of Kylie's brightness and the larger mission her short life has propelled them on.

In *Water Bugs and Dragonflies: Explaining Death to Young Children*, the dragonfly explains why he had to leave the water bugs, where he went and why. He says how wonderful this new world is, but remembers his promise to try to go back to the water bugs. "Well I am just waiting for the other dragonflies to get to this place and then they will understand."

In many ways, Elizabeth is reminded that Kylie is somewhere waiting and watching as well.

Throughout Kylie's treatment, everyone prayed, "I hope you get your miracle for Kylie."

Today, Elizabeth, says she has redefined *miracle*. "Our miracle is that one little life changed so many others. I hold on to that, to the greater purpose," says Elizabeth.

"It has been more than a year since she died, and I continue to experience the long reach of grief in every part of my life," says Elizabeth. "But the pain has lessened, and I have positive memories of the short time I spent with my daughter. I have photographs of her father holding her, of our little family sitting together on the couch in the hospital, and I have the little blue hat that she wore."

The Long family's devotion to soliciting donations stands out. They are not just providing funds but also their expertise. The duo speaks at hospitals regularly, helping to educate health care providers on how to most compassionately work with parents and children—and to deal with their grief too. "We have had doctors tell us that after delivering the bad news to parents, they have gone in a closet to cry, that they have no place to put that pain," says Elizabeth. "We hope that what we went through will help them and help other families."

In spring 2006, the Longs spoke to a group of about 100 doctors and parents associated with Akron Children's hospital.

"We told Kylie's story in hopes that sharing the lessons we all learned would help each doctor treat future patients," says Elizabeth. "Everyone was extremely welcoming and receptive. A few doctors thanked us for sharing our story and promised they would take Kylie's lessons to heart as they treat all their future patients."

Then the parents' group presented the Longs with a framed lithograph that will hang in the Emergency Department with a plaque for Kylie as a visual reminder of her story. They also gave them a card with the picture on it. The title of it was perfect too: *Towards Light.*

"We realized through all this how important it is for parents not to have to worry about anything else except being there for their child," says Elizabeth. "Our foundation is here so hopefully we can take away the things parents have to worry about, like paying electrical bills—the things that would take them away from being with their child. We are determined to turn our grief into purpose."

For more information, contact Elizabeth at the Kylie Jane Long Foundation *(www.kyliejanelong.org)* or at "kylielong" *(www. CarePages.com)*.

Words to Live By

"We told Kylie's story in hopes that sharing the lessons we all learned would help each doctor treat future patients."

Making a Difference to Make Things Better

By Lauren Spiker, Melissa's mom

It is one of the most beautiful compensations of this life that no man can sincerely try to help another without helping himself.
—Ralph Waldo Emerson

"If you have learned anything from me through all of this, do something with it to make a difference—to make things better." These words, spoken by my daughter three days before she died, would become her last request and her lasting legacy for all teens with cancer. They also became the impetus for a new mission that would change the direction of my life.

Melissa was seventeen and a senior in high school when she was diagnosed with a rare bone marrow malignancy. A routine physical exam on a wintry February morning started us down an unexpected path of twisted disappointments and broken dreams on which, despite the sadness, we found the warmth of human compassion and the power of individual spirit.

I will never forget the day we learned Melissa had cancer. In just one minute, with just one word, everything changed. Instead of the Ivy League university to which Melissa had just been accepted, our local children's hospital would become her second home. My sweet daughter—a dancer, a pianist, a scholar, a beauty—would endure two years of debilitating treatment including aggressive chemotherapy, total body radiation, bone marrow transplant, and brain surgery through which I could only watch and hold her hand. I felt so helpless, unable to change the course of events, desperate to trade places if only it were possible. Instead, I spent the days and months watching my daughter find meaning and purpose in every day, focused on what she could do rather than that which she couldn't.

Through it all, the assault of therapy, the isolation of a hospital room, and the frustration of interrupted plans, Melissa kept living. She attended a local university part-time, swam and exercised regularly at the YMCA (with me in tow), and learned new skills like crocheting and pottery making. Each day was a blessing with hope for new tomorrows and a return to our old lives. In the most stressful circumstances imaginable, we found ourselves, mother and daughter, laughing and crying at the same time.

A cure for Melissa's disease, however, was not to be. With all treatment options exhausted, including experimental drug treatment, Melissa made her most courageous decision. Given the option of continued palliative chemotherapy to possibly extend her life a short time, Melissa opted to stop treatment and focus on quality of life over quantity of days. Having accepted that her time on Earth was very limited, Melissa said, "I don't want to die sick." Over the next three months, until she died in June 2000, Melissa made plans for her death and burial, said good-bye to family and friends, and showed us what it meant to live each day as if it were the last. Until the end, Melissa lived the life she had been given courageously, with exceptional grace and untarnished dignity. She died at home, in our arms, at peace, just as she'd hoped, without fear, without pain, without suffering.

In the months following Melissa's death, I wrestled with how to fulfill the promise I had made—"to make a difference, to make things better." During one of many candid conversations before she died, we agreed that her ashes would be buried in a new garden that my husband and I would build in her honor. Preparing Melissa's garden gave my life short-term purpose in those sad days right after Melissa died. While digging sod and raking rocks in our weedy side lawn, I had time to reflect on all that I had learned from my daughter as the July sun burned as brightly as her spirit. I remembered what she said during that late night talk when I told her how proud I was of her and thanked her for all she had taught me. "A lot of people say that to me," she said. "But I'm not sure that everyone will do anything differently because of it. Promise me," she continued, "that if you have learned anything from me through all of this that you will do something with it to make a difference—to make things better." Now I was left pondering, what had I learned and what would I do with it?

The lessons were profound and transformative. Live each day with purpose. Focus your energy on what is really important. Value the love and friendship of others. Advocate for what you know is right. Stay in touch with your inner self. Keep your dreams alive. Seize every opportunity to be creative. Be grateful for gifts received. Never give up hope. Cherish each moment.

Melissa, in a life far too short for my liking, had lived each day exemplifying these simple truths. This was her legacy. My job was to now find a way to use what I had learned. An idea began taking shape along with her garden.

I had seen firsthand the effects of a cancer diagnosis on a teenager and watched as Melissa tried to navigate a health care system not designed for adolescents. Not yet adults and no longer children, teens are often caught in a health care void—somewhere between the juvenile décor of a pediatric facility and the quiet, harsh reality of an adult clinic. They fit neatly into neither. Teens with cancer face unique psychosocial challenges such as the loss of their emerging independence, poor self-image due to disfiguring treatment, isolation and loss of peer support, and diminished sense of control at a time when new boundaries are just being tested. Appropriate resources for this age group were nonexistent when Melissa was sick, with nothing to read in the oncology clinic of our local children's hospital but *Highlights for Children,* as one example. I began to think of ways to support this very vulnerable population and thus was born Melissa's Living Legacy Foundation.

Today, we are proud to boast that the Teens Living with Cancer Web site is the most comprehensive and authoritative Web-based resource for teens with cancer, providing relevant information about their disease and treatment in teen-friendly language, in addition to coping strategies tested by our Teen Advisory Council. Various interactive functions allow teens to connect with others around the globe to form new peer communities and networks of teens and families alike. Our award-winning materials are sent free of charge to all our member hospitals for distribution to their teen patients. Additionally, our clinician workshops, delivered by a team of trained facilitators, are helping health care professionals develop more effective communication and relationship skills with their teen cancer patients.

I am very proud of all that has been accomplished, but more remains to be done for the approximately 15,000 teens in the United States who, like Melissa, endure debilitating treatment for cancer each year. They deserve the very best we can give, though we pray one day our services will no longer be needed. Until then, we must carry on, remembering the lessons Melissa taught us, each in our own way working "to make a difference—to make things better."

For more information go to Teens Living with Cancer at *www.teenslivingwithcancer.org.*

→ Getting Started: The Inside Track on How We Carry Each Other

What we know for sure from our larger CarePages family is that in some way, everyone is a role model for someone else. Whether it is the caregiver who is there 24/7 to help a loved one or friend, or the person who has undergone great adversity in his or her journey to be well, all have reached inside to make a difference in another's life.

We celebrate the actions, big and small, that underscore what our millions of members do every day of their lives. We hope you will join us in applauding them. We thank everyone on these pages for sharing their stories, and we invite you to follow their lead on "how we carry each other."

CHAPTER 10

THE ETIQUETTE OF ILLNESS AND LOSS

What to Say and Do and What *Not* to Say and Do

If you have learned to walk
A little more sure-footedly than I,
Be patient with my stumbling then
And know that only as I do my best and try
May I attain the goal
For which we both are striving.

If through experience, your soul
Has gained heights which I
As yet in dim-lit vision see,
Hold out your hand and point the way,
Lest from its straightness I should stray,
And walk a mile with me.
—Anonymous

Navigating the complex terrain of illness and loss is challenging, to say the least. Drawing on the interviews for this book with people who have been dealing with serious illness and death, we have created a checklist of what we are calling "the etiquette of what to do and what *not* to do" from these true-life experiences.

- Do, call, write, e-mail, and acknowledge that your friend, loved one, family member has a life-threatening disease.
- Don't ignore it.
- Do ask them how they are doing and if they need to talk.
- Do ask them if you can help with driving, shopping, returning calls, helping with their children, making meals.
- Don't take *No* for an answer.
- Do tell them you *love* them and are here for them.
- Don't hide under a rock because *you* are afraid.
- Don't be afraid to touch them. . . . Many illnesses, such as cancer, are *not* contagious. Give them a big hug when you see them.
- Do remember that even if they say they don't need help with any of these things, they *do*. . . . Don't be afraid to just take charge.
- Do send cards, notes and flowers and make phone calls to encourage them to be positive and let them know you care.

✢ Don't give up on them — they need you.

✢ Do call people when you know they are sick. Find out a time that works best for the caregiver. Some patients sleep in the morning, others in the night. Try to find out the patient's schedule.

✢ Don't expect the caregiver to call you back. The caregiver has everything they can do to be there for the patient, so at the end of the day, you can't have the expectation that they will call or e-mail you back.

✢ Don't take it personally if a caregiver snaps at you. Keep in mind the burdens they are carrying and know that stress, sleep deprivation, emotions, and other factors are weighing heavily on them.

✢ Do listen . . . and don't feel you have to offer advice.

CONCLUSION

Seize the Opportunity to Help

There is no ending to these stories. Everyday it seems we will wake up and life will hand us treasures and challenges. Loss and illness sometimes break into our ordinary days in a heartbeat and our worlds are thrown upside down. As Dana Reeve said shortly before her own death, "I learned a long time ago life isn't fair. . . . you just forge ahead."

This book is a collection of stories of lives that have met extraordinary challenges and the indelible mark they have left on the lives of the friends and families who have been called on to step up to care. Some people reading this book might say that life is too hard, we shouldn't have to deal with all of this. But we will say that interviewing all of the people here, one message rang loud and clear: When you care, when you reach inside yourself to reach out to another, when we carry each other, it changes everything. Somewhere, there is someone who needs *you* to reach out and say, "You are not alone."

Our hope is that you will be inspired to care and take action. "All you need is deep within you waiting to unfold and reveal itself," reminds Eileen Caddy of the Finhorn Community of Scotland.

And if there is any question about how caring and love bubble up and overflow, consider these words from our friend Pam, whose life was changed in one second when a car barreled into her and her husband's SUV on a sunny Spring day last May:

"The small acts of kindness have all been so important to us, giving us strength and assurance that all is right with our world. I am getting stronger and the pain is getting less. Each day I spend a little time saying a prayer in thanksgiving that Bill and I survived the crash, that our son and his friend were not in the car (for they would have perished), and for the countless blessings we have received from God, our family, our caregivers, and our friends. Each new sunrise, day's events, people connection, and new sunset are viewed with a changed vision, one of hope, thanksgiving and wonder."

We carry each other because we need to, because we need others to know they are not alone.

RESOURCE CENTER

We mention important resources in the text. To make it easy for you to find them, we offer their contact information below:

In Chapter 4, Connection, you met Bonnie Addario. To find out more about the Bonnie J. Addario Lung Cancer Foundation, check out *www.abreathawayfromthecure.org*.

In Chapter 6, Give What You Have, you met hypnotherapist Kerstin Sjoquist. Kerstin's "Bliss Trips" CDs can be ordered on-line at *www.blisstrips.com*. You also met Hollywood makeup artist extraordinaire Lori Ovitz. Lori's book, *Facing the Mirror with Cancer*, can be ordered through Belle Press, *www.facingthemirror.org*.

Another wonderful resource for those in the caring community is the not-for-profit Flower Power, which delivers flower arrangements to hospices, nursing homes, and hospitals. You can find them online at *www.flowerpowerfoundation.org*.

In Chapter 8, Caring for the Caregiver, Kevin E. O'Connor, CSP, talks about creating a caring community among siblings. Kevin O'Connor is a professional speaker, consultant, and pastoral counselor and educator at Loyola University in Chicago. He can be contacted through *www.kevinoc.com* or *www.kevinbureau.com*.

There are, of course, many, many books out there on grief and loss. A few that we would particularly recommend are:

Chodron, Pema, *The Places That Scare You: A Guide to Fearlessness in Difficult Times* (Boston, MA: Shambhala, 2001).

Hickman, Martha W., *Healing After Loss: Daily Meditations For Working Through Grief* (New York: Collins Publishers, 1999).

Hope, Lori, *Help Me Live: 20 Things People With Cancer Want You to Know* (Berkeley, CA: Celestial Arts, 2005).

Kuner, Susan, with Carol Orsborn, Linda Quigley, and Karen Stroup, *Speak the Language of Healing: Living With Breast Cancer Without Going to War* (Berkeley, CA: Conari Press, 1999).

Kushner, Harold, *When Bad Things Happen to Good People*, by Harold Kushner (New York: Avon, 1983).

Noel, Brook and Pamela Blair, *I Wasn't Ready to Say Goodbye: Surviving, Coping and Healing After the Death of a Loved One* (Belgium, WI: Champion Press, 2000).

O'Connor, Nancy, *Letting Go With Love: The Grieving Process* (La Mariposa Press, Tucson, AZ: 1994).

You can also find a regularly updated list of resources at our Web site, *www.CarePages.com*, including the "We Carry Each Other: What to Say and What to Do When Someone You Love is Ill or Has Suffered Loss" Resource Center, the "We Carry Each Other" blog hosted by author Mary Beth Sammons, and a menu of disease-specific Emotional Resource Centers that provide the caring component to illness.

ABOUT THE AUTHORS

Eric Langshur is cofounder and CEO of TLContact, Inc., a Chicago-based healthcare service company that created and maintains *CarePages.com*, a Web site where family and friends can communicate and form communities of support when a loved one is receiving medical care. More than 550 health-care facilities across the United States and Canada, including Johns Hopkins Hospital and Health System, The Mayo and Cleveland Clinics, and Massachusetts General Hospital, also offer enhanced, customized, and secure versions of CarePages as an extension of their patient services (*www.CarePages.com*). Active in the community, Eric serves on the board of the National Family Caregivers Association in Washington, D.C., and is a Trustee of Big Brothers-Big Sisters of Connecticut. He lives in Chicago with his wife, Sharon, and their three young children.

Sharon Langshur has an extensive and varied background in the healthcare field. Prior to forming TLContact with her husband Eric, Sharon worked as a pediatric resident at Children's Memorial Hospital in Chicago. In addition, Sharon has done extensive research on human genetics and has served as a genetic counselor. She lives in Chicago with her husband and their three young children.

Mary Beth Sammons is an award-winning journalist, author, and cause-marketing specialist whose work appears frequently in the *Chicago Tribune, Family Circle, Parents, Cooking Light, www.beliefnet.com,* and McGraw-Hill trade publications. She is the author of six books, including *Gifts with Heart* (Conari 2002). She lives with three teenage children in the Chicago suburbs.

TO OUR READERS